CORRUPTION REIGNS IN OUR COURTROOMS

Musical Genius Concepts, Inc.
PO Box 172
Woodbury, New York 11797

www.missgloriaparker.com

ISBN-13: 978-0-9788136-0-4
ISBN-10: 0-9788136-0-X

Printed in the United States of America

Dedication

I dedicate this book to the memory of my beautiful mother, Rose, who was a great inspiration in all my various talents, and to my father, who helped make it all possible, with his loving kindness.

Disclaimer

Everything I say in this book, I have lived through in the American Court System. This, is my opinion of my plight seeking justice at the hands of these lawyers and Judges that I had business dealings with. These are my thoughts and my experiences.

And this, is a mere sampling of what goes on in our Courts today.

Her poetry, like her
music, comes
naturally. "Once I get
an inspiration
something happens
and the words just flow",
she said. "They are sincere,
not contrived songs."
Her success and dedication
is also a result of a
highly disciplined upbringing.

The man, who has bought the power To wield this hammer, in his Black Robes of attire, and is not forthright To his oath, could be, and is, The ultimate degradation and devistation of humanity.

CORRUPTION REIGNS IN OUR COURTROOMS

"The reason I wrote this book is because I have suffered four times in the court system as a plaintiff with these Judges and lawyers. My experience with their possible corruption has inspired this book."

Yes, as a plaintiff, Pro Se, in several cases, seeking my rights that were stolen from me by those who had connections and who probably manipulate the laws, to serve their friends and compatriots. Unfortunately, the black robes that cover their sins on the bench, also gives one who wears it, Carte Blanche to probably play God. And yet, this is happening to many who go to court placing their trust in their lawyers, and the presiding Judge, to seek a just solution to their case, and never to find it. But, I have been endowed with this musical talent and foresight as my vehicle, and after several of my law actions have been probably manipulated and also possibly massacred at the hands of those addressed as, "Your Honor", my songs and my lyrics and experiences, I hope, will help you all who have not had your day of justice, to know...

"You are Not Alone"

PREFACE

EVIL LURKS IN THESE BUILDINGS WHERE MEN DON ROBES OF BLACK AND DEFY GOD

THESE BUILDINGS ARE CALLED COURT HOUSES, OR MORE APPROPRIATELY— "BROTHELS!"

The United States has the dubious distinction of being the **ONLY** nation in the world with the **MAXIMUM NUMBER OF ATTORNEYS PER CAPITA.** Do you wonder **WHY?** Because the Judges and lawyers have a common objective, the maximization of income **WITHOUT RESTRAINT,** and we, are just the hapless victims. Those who write the laws in the United States Congress or in State Houses are themselves lawyers, who make the laws to protect their business' and their own interests, and the Press in the United States do not inform the public for **OBVIOUS** reasons!

And so, this book and songs were born as a result of the **SYSTEMATIC MISCARRIAGE OF JUSTICE IN BOTH,** the Federal and New York State Courts.

Now, I do not say all Judges and Lawyers are dishonest, but my experiences in 4 cases here in New York have awakened me and alerted me to the deal making and goings on with my then lawyers-and also with me being a Pro-Se **(attorney for myself.)** To see justice **manipulated** and **thwarted** first hand – in America – has truly shocked me. Now, if I had not witnessed the lying and the **skullduggery,** - I would not have believed it. But I have seen this unfold before me in this sick Court system, from **TOP** – **TO** – **BOTTOM.**

I found, in my experience on the Federal level, it is the unchecked usurpation of legislative powers by the judiciary, and there are no mechanisms of government to detect the **unlawful** acts of the **Federal Judiciary** and the **corrupt practices** rampant in the **State Courts. JUDGES ARE PART OF THE POLITICAL SYSTEM,** as are **LAWYERS.**

Only today did I get an answer back from a letter I sent to the Attorney General of New York State. The reply finally came some three months after my letter to him. So, after waiting this **lengthy, anxious, time,** this is the answer I got from one of his underlings. **"YOU MAY WISH TO CONSULT AN ATTORNEY – THE NASSAU COUNTY BAR ASSOCIATION WILL BE PLEASED TO PROVIDE YOU WITH AN APPROPRIATE REFERRAL."** He even gave me the phone numbers to call.

SO YOU SEE HOW THEY WORK – HAND IN HAND AND WALLET TO WALLET!

A CLARIFICATION

****

THIS BOOK DOES NOT ADDRESS OUR ENTIRE COURT SYSTEM. IT DEALS WITH DISHONESTY AND CROOCKEDNESS TOWARDS ME, AND I AM SURE TOWARDS THOUSANDS AND THOUSANDS OF VICTIMS WHO KEEP FALLING INTO THE SAME TRAP.

****

TABLE OF CONTENTS

-

KARMA

-**KARMA**- The influence of an individual's past actions on his future lives and reincarnations.

-In the chain of lives, an individual can perfect himself or degrade himself in such an Evil way that he is reborn as an animal.

-**KARMA** is regarded as the universal chain of **'Cause and Effect'** and **Birth and Death.**

-Not only do past acts influence the circumstances of the next life, they also determine one's happiness or unhappiness.

CHAPTER ONE

"THERE IS A REASON FOR <u>EVERYTHING</u> ~AND, <u>EVERYTHING</u> ~ HAS A REASON...."

A Bird's eye view of your cruelty to me, and Your eventual **KARMA.....**

-Is it not Strange?....Read on.....

- Had my mother ***not*** been a great violinist and ***not*** started me on my first instrument a quarter size violin, at 3 1/2 years of age.

- Had my mother ***not*** given me all the musical knowledge and background and lessons with the finest musical teachers.

- Had the Glaser office (the Great theatrical Agent,) ***not*** caught my concert, and ***not engage*** me to conduct the all girl orchestra that he brought in from out west when I was a teenager.

- Had ***not*** the great musical arranger, **ALPHONSE D'ARTEGA** ***not*** been engaged to rehearse the orchestra with one of his famous compositions, **<u>"In The Blue of Evening",</u>** while we were at the Nola Studios on Broadway in New York preparing for a tour across the country.

- Had ***not*** Local 802, American Federation of Musicians, printed in it's directory listing the famous conductor **D'ARTEGA,** residing on Staten Island.

- Had I ***not*** called the phone number listed, and **Bernard** S. answered sadly, advising me that **D'ARTEGA** was ***not available,*** and that he had passed away recently.

- Had **Bernard *not*** come to visit me to tell me about **D'ARTEGA** and his music with the Church since he became a Priest.

- Had Bernard ***not*** wanted to marry me.

Had **Bernard *not*** slipped back into ***drinking*** for that *one* ***month in January,*** when **TWO NEW WILLS** were drawn up by the **Lawyer and Secretary** within 10 days, while his ***senses were impaired by the liquor.***

We all would ***not*** be brought together ***here and now,*** because of the **manipulated WILLS.** You have all; **each and everyone of you,** involved in this ***'catastrophic'*** case earned your **'KARMIC'** debt, because of your ***cruel treatment and lies to me.***

First let me fill you in on my last case in the courts. It is this type of conduct and the manipulations of the Judges and the lawyers in our court system, that shall we say, inspired me to relate the goings on that I had to put up with, in ***this most disgusting case.***

The lawyers I had engaged for several of my cases as a Plaintiff, and the lawyers and Judges that I dealt with, when I handled the other two cases **MYSELF AS A PRO-SE (a lawyer representing myself)** made me see and learn just what goes on first hand of how, ***'fixed and corrupt'*** **most of** our court system truly is.

And it is for this reason that I am writing this book, so the people who have to do business with these ***legal-ites,*** are to be very careful who they engage, and to watch every step that they make.

You really ***cannot be too careful*** when choosing the right attorney. Most of them are so ***devious,*** they know every trick in the book, **(those that they never take off the shelf.)** Their only way of thinking is how long can they drag this case out, and how much money can they **(SUCK)** out of you.

The lawyers on both sides meet and they plan ***their strategies.*** They figure out how much ***money*** you have, how ***anxious*** you are, and how long to keep your case going. They even have conferences with the Judge. Then *all* ***three*** plan their ***little charade!***

This exact situation happened to me and is now happening to some friends of mine. Their case is already into the 4th. year. Because they have money, the Judge and the lawyers are hanging on. You see these legal ones cannot lose. They have threatened to take ***their home, their business*** and several ***other things.*** Whichever way these people turn, ***they lose!*** It has taken a terrible toll on their lives. The case is in a ***Stalemate!***

The Bar Association will not do anything to help. Why should they? **THEY** are ***all lawyers too***. Yes-it is a ***sad day*** in America that this legal business is so out of control. And there is ***no one*** to turn to, for help.

Now I would like to fill you in on this last case that brought me to this point to write about. This ***experience*** has left me in this position to seek some relief from this ***corruption.* It *absolutely has to be brought out*** for the Public to be made aware of.

Do not let them intimidate you. Keep notes of all that they say. And remember the lawyer, is ***not your best friend,*** although they may try to win your confidence, **be on your guard.**

And now I will go on with this last case that gave me the incentive to write about, and how **THEIR KARMA** will be involved and will take over for these people in the American Court System, who are possibly in it **only for the money they can cheat from you.**

~And as we say – **"THE BEST IS YET TO COME."** You may as well ask yourselves, "How did this all come about?" Well ***now*** you know. The Gods have been testing you, and how better? For what *you* have done to *me* in this ***Surrogate case is shamefully dishonest!*** To think you can graduate with the **title Lawyer** and ***practice in subterfuges.***

I can search my **conscience.** I have only done the right thing to people and animals that have crossed my path, or come into my life. This is my background. My parents instilled this ***honesty and kindness*** in me as a way of life when I was growing up. So this shock of ***chicanery*** and the ***burying of the facts and truths are Ungodly and Sinful.***

Bernard had stopped **drinking** and **smoking** for all the while he knew us. I made it quite plain to him from the start that **I do not allow smoking and drinking in my home** because of my animals. My African Grey

Parrots, and I are both allergic to the smoke. He agreed, and he would come out every weekend from his home on Staten Island. He brought some of **D'ARTEGA'S** ***recordings-and a tape he made with this great Leader about a story on*** **ALCOHOLISM** which he both wrote and narrated with the beautiful music and arrangements, of **D'ARTEGA** and his Orchestra.

Well, as the fates would have it, we had a great snowstorm in the beginning of January 1999. I lost all my electricity. No heat, no cooking and it was cold. I moved my Parrots and the rest of my pets into my large den. My wood burning fire place had to make do to warm us. My orchestra manager did his best to bring in wood from my property to keep us from freezing, which was not an easy chore.

I told **Bernard** it would not be advisable to make the trip from his home in Staten Island to my home on Long Island because the roads were too icy, and that I live on a hill and it would just be too dangerous. Besides the fact that I had **NO HEAT.** So he stayed home.

He had a young tenant who lived upstairs who would play loud **Rock** and **Roll** records, and who would have parties on the weekends while **Bernard** was not at home. **Bernard** called me the first night and told me he could not stand the ***noise,*** and the running up and down the stairs of the tenants friends. He said the loud music was really getting him mad, and he asked the tenant to **"quiet down."**

When I called him later that evening I was ***Shocked***. **He** ***did not recognize my voice.*** He asked "***Who is this?"*** His voice was ***garbled,*** and he was **NOT** himself. After ***months of Sobriety he had slipped and gone back to drinking!***

In his **FIRST WILL** made on **May 26, 1998,** I was named as the ***Executrix.*** He also gave me **copies of Double E Bonds with my name on them P.O.D. in the amount of $300,000. Bernard also stated in the WILL his wishes were to have his Church Services in his Church in Brooklyn, and he wanted HIS HOUSE DONATED TO HIS CHURCH.** Since he was in the Air Force, he wished to be buried in Pinelawn National Cemetery, these wishes were *very* ***important*** *to* **Bernard** because he was in the service.

When Bernard ***slipped and began drinking again,*** **his** lawyer, knowing that he had **no living relatives took complete advantage of the situation. He quickly contrived a NEW WILL on January 19, 1999 and** ***took me off as Executrix, and made HIMSELF Executor.*** And, on **January 29,1999,** ***10 days later*** made **ANOTHER WILL** *cutting me down and putting his* ***SECETARY IN FOR 25%!*** He also ***cut out Bernard's Church, a Church where all the members of his family were buried.***

Later that year **Bernard** passed away on November 6, 1999. This so called ***Executor*** did so many ***illegal*** things with **Bernard's WILL,** it would take volumes to relate it to you. **INCLUDING FORGERY!**

All I've ever said to **Bernard** was, ***"You will live a good healthy life if you stay away from*** the **SMOKING AND DRINKING."** He told my manager, who would also spend the weekends with us that he was a, **"Two Fisted Drinker,"** a habit which he developed while he was in the Air Force.

I had ***never been to*** **Bernard's** house on ***Staten Island***, so when the lawyer told me to come to the ***courthouse 45 days later, I said, "Take us to Bernard's House*** while we are here***. He did not want to but I insisted***, so he took us. **HE OPENED THE DOOR <u>AND HE FLED</u>!!!**

No small wonder! I was ***stunned***! I was in ***shock***! It looked as if a ***Tornado had gone through the House***. Clothing was ***strewn all over***, ***drawers*** were opened, ***socks*** and ***underwear*** were ***heaped*** on the floor-it was ***Impossible to Navigate***. The first thing that ***alerted*** me was that the <u>**T.V.**</u> was ***sorely missing***. What I saw were the chairs where **Bernard** and **D'ARTEGA** would sit and watch T.V. together and an empty T.V. table. I cannot in a million words express to you the ***shambles*** his place was *left in*. Not ***one drawer*** closed – things ***hanging out!*** When I saw the **beautiful Crucifixes** on the floors, I could not understand the ***barbaric people who could do this.*** The ***neighbors*** next door and this ***lawyer*** were the ***only ones*** with the *Keys* to **Bernard's** House.

And, there was something else. **Bernard** was very concerned about the Y2K, the run on the Banks and all the possible problems that could occur, so he purchased a ***safe and put $25,000 in it preparing for the '2000' Rush!*** He also ***purchased a very expensive Rifle*** which he had to apply specifically for a gun license. He stocked up on ***food, water, flashlights etc.*** The **SAFE** and **STRONG BOX (which I had gotten a receipt for both)** were missing. ***When I questioned, the Public Administrator, at length later, about the whereabouts of the safe, I was told the safe was indeed in the house,***

however it had a large hole through the top of it, and it was empty. Where did the $25,000 plus and all of Bernard's Jewelry disappear to? And, who took his ***lawn mower, snow blower, rifle and exercise equipment?*** The thievery was on a Grand scale. The only people to have the use of the keys to **Bernard's** house, were ***the next door neighbor, and his lawyer.***

Can you imagine this ***dishonorable Executive*** immediately putting a **'FOR SALE'** sign on the House? I told the Judge that it was **VERY WRONG,** and that it was to go to **BERNARD'S FAMILY CHURCH WHERE HIS WHOLE FAMILY WENT,** as was stated in his **FIRST WILL.** It was ***so very dishonest what they were doing....selling a house which Bernard had WILLED to his CHURCH.*** It does not get much lower than that.

Yes, dishonesty ***flourished*** in that courthouse. And to this day **NO ONE WILL GIVE ME ANY ANSWERS....The Public Administrator, The Judge, the entire court system-NO ONE!**

A handwriting Expert who I hired, said in his report that **"ONLY THE 1ST WILL WAS BERNARD'S "SIGNATURE," WHICH WAS DATED MAY 26, 1998. THE SIGNATURES ON THE OTHER TWO WILLS WERE NOT BERNARD'S SIGNATURE, BUT RATHER FORGERIES.**

The *lawyer/Executor/Will writer with his wife* did not play fair with me. They knew that **Bernard** had **NO relatives....NO ONE** to question what they had done with the **TWO NEW WILLS.** It was **A TOTAL CHARADE!** Each of you together who have

perpetrated this farce, this **illegal subterfuge,** seemed to have done it possibly with the ***Courts Blessings.*** You all **aided and abetted each other**, and for that ***YOU, will all pay.***

Everything equals out. You will realize what you did to me. The Lord will **NOT** be set aside! All I wanted was ***the truth and justice from that court.*** **You lied *under oath on the Witness Chair. You shouted me Down!*** Your ***plotting*** in the hall of the Courthouse (**that most Unholy place.) A** place probably soaked ***with lies, trickery, deals and deceit.***

You were ***All very likely coached on how NOT to say a word*** *about* **BERNARD'S DRINKING**. ***The EXECUTOR engaged the Ex-Judge who sat on that very same bench before this present Judge of two years. So, after he sat there for fifteen years and now went in as a lawyer,*** he was engaged by the **EXECUTOR** ***not to say a word about Bernard's ALCOHOLISM!***

The **TWO WILLS** which were dated ***10 days apart*** were evidently done while **Bernard** was ***intoxicated*** that month in ***January in 1999,*** and he was **NOT AWARE OF THE CHANGES. The sitting Judge of TWO years told the Executor he should engage a lawyer. Would you believe he gets *this Ex-Judge (whose picture hangs high on the wall in the courtroom, who warmed that very same bench for 15 years!)***

Since I am ***Pro Se*** Attorney in this case (I will not engage a lawyer for myself as **I DO NOT TRUST THEM!** I had to question all these witnesses; The Executor, his wife, **the secretary who typed all THE WILLS** **(LEAVING OUT PROVISION #4 IN THE**

2ND AND 3RD WILLS, ***deceitful*** people, I could not believe it. And when the ***results*** of this **PUTNAM HEARING** was printed, it was possibly the **Ex-Judge who wrote it and the sitting Judge probably signed it without even reading it.**

Now, Mr. Lombardi, my Orchestra Manager who spent every weekend with **Bernard,** told the Court that **"BERNARD TOLD HIM THAT HE WAS AN ALCOHOLIC."** He spoke under oath on the witness chair, answering ***all of my questions unrehearsed.***

The Judge commended him saying, **"YOU WERE THE BEST WITNESS HERE- THANK YOU FOR COMING."** Yet...*He was* **NOT** at all mentioned of taking the witness stand, **AS IF HE WAS NEVER EVEN IN THAT COURTROOM.... CAN YOU IMAGINE, THEY ARE TRYING TO HIDE THE FACT THAT BERNARD WAS AN ALCOHOLIC?** Why do you think that was??? Because they did not want the **PUBLIC TO KNOW** that ***Bernard*** was an ***Alcoholic*** and belonged to **AA,** and that the **TWO WILLS** were made when he **WAS DRINKING.** I made sure, I bought **THAT TRANSCRIPT!**

What the **puzzle** is, the ***Court covered this all up.*** How can you leave a **Provision #4 out of a WILL,** when it was in the **1ST. WILL? Provisions 1,2,3 and 5 were all there....where was Provision #4??** How can you make the **SAME ERROR TWICE** – **(in the 2nd. And 3rd. WILLS?)** The answer is no one ever checked it. **Bernard** was never even aware of ***it's existence,*** and it was **INTENTIONALLY LEFT OUT** in order to possibly benefit themselves. If **Bernard** ever saw those **WILLS HE NEVER WOULD HAVE SIGNED**

THEM. NO NEVER!! THE CHURCH WAS TOO IMPORTANT TO HIM AND HIS FAMILY.....A **HANDWRITING EXPERT,** who studied the **TWO WILLS** and many of the cards and letters that **Bernard** had sent me, stated for the record that the **TWO WILLS** of **January 19th. and 29th. WERE NOT HIS HANDWRITING!**

So, now you know your lies ***did not*** hurt me. You all put your ***necks*** in the ***noose.*** You signed your own ticket with **THE DEVIL,** and for what you've done to **BERNARD and ME**, you have probably ***registered your own*** **KARMA,** and sadly ***your*** loved ones will ***suffer*** for what you **deliberately have done to me, under oath, in the Halls** ***of the Courthouse.***

I am truly glad this ordeal is over. I must forget this, ***'NIGHTMARE ON STATEN ISLAND'**, and this miserable episode in my life. The only good that has come out of this whole fiasco is that I am exposing to the world, **THE DISHONESTY, THE DECEIT, THE MANIPULATION OF THE UNJUST COURT SYSTEM** ***in Our Beautiful Country that our Forefathers gave us and left to us.***

AS FOR ALL OF YOU, WHO DESECRATED ME , YOU HAVE HAD THE <u>HONOR</u> TO MEET A TRULY TALENTED LADY.....BUT NOW THE SUNLIGHT SHINES BRIGHT. I KNOW THE TRUTH! AND GOD KNOWS THE TRUTH...... AND...I HAVE LEARNED FIRST HAND THE SORDED LIFE IN SURROGATE'S COURT,

AND THE RATS THAT INHABIT IT WERE ALL GROVELING FOR THAT SMALL PIECE....OF STINKING CHEESE!!

Nightmare on Staten Island
Dear Readers, this would make a Great title for a Movie!

CHAPTER-TWO

"AT LAST"

So, here we are at this junction in my life. A life filled with studies, music, performing for audiences, a family filled with love and devotion, and doing God's work for people and animals.

And what a ***junction*** it is for me, who is trying to find justice in the **American Court System,** which is in many ways ***plagued*** with ***dishonesty, greed, self serving Judges and lawyers,*** and anything that is ***vile*** and that comes into mind.

To think that I have kept this **court manipulated case** alive for over **three years.** Each and every person involved here who has ***thwarted*** the truths that I have tried to bring forth. **I have the proofs, the bills of sale, the stealing, pilfering cover ups,** and **yet not one living soul** has come forth to agree with my accusations. Oh, how they covered up for one another **to hide the *facts, to lie, to steal, to huddle together, plot and plan how to cheat me*** and sadly yet, with the possible ***condonation of his holy one,*** **THE JUDGE!**

The time has come, **PARADE REST!** I know for sure why **The Lord** wanted me in this case of ***this friend*** who passed away and the Lawyers who ***massacred his WILLS.*** It was ***no accident.*** It was **premeditated,** ***the public*** must be made aware of the goings on ***in the court system and if I am the chosen one to do it, so be it***.

You all showed *your **true colors!*** **YOU** who have swept ***the truth*** under those dirty floors, **(there already is enough of that in this courtroom)** and I have now reached this pinnacle. The Judge is now holding ***me in contempt.*** After all **who am I? A Pro Se** who was ***telling the truth begging for the truth,*** which is very likely ***forbidden*** in the court system. The ***manipulating lawyers*** are the only ones to cavort in these ***sick lying cases*** with the Judge. ***What right*** do I have to ***seek the truth, to tell the truth,*** oh no, not in these apparently **predetermined court deals.** The deals that are fomented only between **the Judge** and **the lawyers on both sides**, as how to split the spoils and possibly include the **BLACK ROBED** one too. So I can see my billing on a Marquee, **"GLORIA PARKER,"** held in **CONTEMPT FOR TELLING THE TRUTH.** Well our dear Lord will handle this for me, because each person in that courtroom that works for the Judge, ***all his henchmen*** that were invited in to witness the job he did on me are possibly ***just as guilty.*** They and their families and their loved ones will pay that heavy price for the ***falsehoods*** and **cover-ups**, and **lies** that were perpetrated on me. One by one, ***each*** will probably ***pay*** and ***suffer*** for what they were part of, and what they were **witness to,** in his **courtroom,** only because I **dared to tell the truth.**

I now for sure realize that ***the court system buries the truth.*** This has been proven to me several times. When my **then lawyers** in other cases were **paid off** to throw my bona fide case for some deal they made with the Judge and other lawyers in their private **clubs-chambers** and **meetings**.

The Lord put me in this case as a ***catalyst,*** and apparently these **thieves** put their own necks in a ***noose.*** The more they hurt me, they will suffer **ten fold over.** All I ever wanted was the ***truth.*** The many letters I wrote to the Judge telling him of the ***robbing and stealing*** of my ***friend's house and monies,*** went un-noticed. He would not listen or answer. They had ***carte blanche*** to do what they did **WITH apparently the *Judge's blessings.*** While the Judge stood by without reprimanding them, ***THEY massacred and thwarted the truth.***

AND FOR THAT the Judge is holding **ME** in ***contempt***. Remember this day well, when you and yours will be repaid for what you all have done to me, **an honest respectable person.** All I wanted was the ***truth!***

You also left the **name** and **testimony** out of your **PUTNAM HEARING** of ***Mr. Lombardi*** who knew the deceased very well. **BECAUSE MR LOMBARDI TOLD THE TRUTH ABOUT WHAT HE KNEW, HIS NAME WAS NOT TO BE MENTIONED. EVEN THOUGH THE JUDGE TOLD HIM, "YOU WERE THE BEST WITNESS HERE TODAY-THANK YOU FOR COMING!"** ***Yet he was not acknowledged or mentioned as being there or present. Your cover up,*** **YOUR HONOR, *is a sick, dishonest move.***

And so-because I dared to tell **the truth** by asking why ***Mr. Lombardi's testimony was deleted,*** **I AM HELD IN "CONTEMPT."**

Well, I've got news for you and yours. When the **DEVIL** paints a big **'C' on your face and chest**, which you will carry for the rest of time into **eternity,** you will **remember the *day you said that contempt word to me,*** **YOUR HONOR .....**

In all my days, I have never entertained a situation that I was involved with that was possibly so duplicitous, but that word is quite synonymous with ***the dealings in***

this court system. I can readily see you all probably have ***no difficulty*** living ***lie after lie.*** **Do not** try to pull me into your web. No, I will not be part of ***your apparent underhanded dealings***, and I will **NOT SIGN** your paper, if it does not have an honest statement about my **deceased friend.** You cannot convince me because I have to live with ***my conscience.***

So now I await the closing of this case. The education I received in this obviously ***corrupt cover up*** was quite a lesson. If I had retained a lawyer, it would have been over **three years ago.** Yet it took a **Pro Se** to possibly find you out, and to ***show the world*** what goes on in a system so ***rampant with dishonesty and disgust and no respect for God!! You did not frighten me or scare me with your*** **CONTEMPT CHARGE.** You only put that noose tighter around **your necks,** and all those who **YES** you and back you up with your tactics.

I somehow feel flattered for what I put you all through. The pain, the anger, the anguish, the nightmares were too much for me to bear, and I could see you did not know or care to play fair with me! Did you all realize that **I WAS A CATALYST?** Did you know that the Lord had me in this case to bring out **your EVILNESS?** Through the years you all got away with **your crooked dealings** and no one ***dared to tell it as it is.*** But **little me,** I stood up to you all. Could you not see the part I played so ***your true colors would come out?***

I GAVE YOU EVERY POSSIBLE CHANCE TO BE HONEST BUT YOU INSULTED ME, YOU LIED TO ME, YOU EVEN CHEATED ME. YOU WILL NOT HAVE ANY PLEASURE FOR HOW YOU TREATED ME. REMEMBER MY WORDS, YOU BROUGHT ALL THIS ON YOURSELVES.

EACH OF YOU AND YOUR DISHONEST GAINS, WILL BE SHORT LIVED, YOU PROBABLY WILL NOT ENJOY ONE MOMENT OF PLEASURE AFTER THIS IS ALL OVER!!!

~~~~ GOOD LUCK TO YOU ALL!

YOU WILL NEED IT! ~~~~

CHAPTER-THREE

"CATALYST-- GLORIA PARKER"

I have ***wondered*** and ***queried,*** **"Why me dear Lord?"** Why was I, and why am I subjected to this **"NIGHTMARE ON STATEN ISLAND?"-** So distant a trip, so early in the morn, before I leave home to go to this place where ***the lies fly free*** and ***undaunted?***

I at least make sure my African Grey Parrots have all the variety of foods to nourish them for the day, **(fresh water, boiled and cooled,)** vitamins, fresh veggies and their cups overflowing with the finest seed and raw peanuts that are flown up from the South. In my back yard, I have another **battalion of Blue Jays, Robbins, Humming Birds, Nuthatches, Cardinals, a Woodpecker** and **his wife,** and every feathered friend that find the **Parker Restaurant** on Long Island- a haven. On my front Terrace, we cater to another variety including **chipmunks and squirrels.** At evening time, I have some beautiful **red foxes** and a **family of raccoons** to fill out the little friends who have made my home their home too.

Once the Lord's little friends are ***adopted*** and stay in ***my home overnight,*** they will never roam the outside to be in harms way. They are fed the best of ***proper foods*** and ***are taken care of and loved.***

Aside from my music, all my instruments that I perform with and **my orchestra, my writings, sewing, designing the clothes I wear on stage and daily,** and **my cooking and baking,** I am very much aware of the additives and preservatives that our foods are laced with, so I try to avoid them and do most of my cooking from start and use only ***natural ingredients.***

~ And so with this case on Staten Island, I drive to this ***foreign unfriendly courthouse,*** where a friend bequeathed a gift of some sort and the ***vultures*** who have ***descended*** to ***feast*** on this person's ***carcass,*** since his passing.

I wonder ***why*** I was, …. ***Yes me*** …. with all my kindness and love for our dear Lord's earthlings, ***why*** was I put into this ***miserable role*** to find Justice in this sick court system - A system with ***so many possible manipulations*** of the American language, a system with so many varied choices. Take anyone that ***fits*** **your** position, that ***permits*** so wide a decision. Why I truly feel that the laws set forth in a court room, are ***tailor made!***

These ***lawyers*** and ***Judges*** can turn an **'IF', 'AND' OR 'BUT'** into a ***variety of interpretations.*** Whichever fits their case. I now know for ***sure*** what my role or performance in this sick world of ***'Jurist Prudence'*** or corruption was meant for. I would like to say it is a ***sick joke*** or a ***bad dream,*** but I am awake, and it is ***not funny.***

After all, what right do I have, me, as a **Pro Se,** to expect the truth, to possibly mess up their **NEATLY CORRUPTED AGENDA,** me, not a lawyer at all, to keep this case alive for over **three years?** With all these ***adversaries, lying their hearts out,*** who am I? - **The bone in their throats** that was keeping them from their ***undeserved*** **"BOUNTY"!**

The fact that their ***contrivances*** and their ***shenanigans*** are running rampant is certain proof that the **DEVIL** is working his points with these possible

mutineers of justice! I do not believe that a good person in a righteous frame of mind could or would in their wildest dream carry on this **'charade,'** with the blessings and the condemnation of those in command and control.

It is ***they*** who are **steering this ship** and doing these ***EVIL*** acts. What shocks me the most is the way they go about their business as if it is normal, their ***subterfuges***.

~ And this is the courtroom scenario: one of these culprit witnesses goes to the ***witness*** chair on ***the Judges right*** that ***most infamous chair,*** which is also ***right in front*** of our ***American flag*** **(that so much Young Blood of our innocent youth shed to uphold.)** Then these witnesses put their hands on the **Holy Bible** and swear ***to tell the truth, etc***., then sit down on **THAT CHAIR** on the judges right, and **LIE, LIE, LIE.**

Now I have unquestionable proof, billings, dates, verification that the answers to the questions I propounded, all of them-**yes-they are all lies!** I have positive proof right in my papers in my hand. It is **SHOCKING,** it is **STUNNING**. But, it is reality. I am not surprised. These varmints apparently have passed the American Bar and so they have **Carte Blanche** to lie under the flag and at the Judges right and after swearing oath on the Bible in that most ***unholy chair.***

This, to me, who was brought up with the greatest respect for ***the Bible,*** for ***the American Flag,*** and you should excuse me, the integrity of the court system, is truly a ***rude awakening!***

Living through this disgusting episode of what I was going through in this surrogate case on Staten Island, and watching this possibly ***disgustingly tainted***

manipulation of the truth made me sick. This occupational disease, **SEEING** how anything goes-***lie to the hilt, flag or no flag, Bible or no Bible.*** Oh yes, because once you pass the bar **(which they should get hit on the head with)** the sky is the limit. Do whatever it takes to win a case. The story is priceless.

~And so it goes. **The Black Robed Bandits** who have apparently relinquished their souls to the ***Devils Brethren.*** This ***putrid stench*** which permeates each courthouse and is the ***degradation*** of ***humanity,*** tarnishes ***ALL that is good!***

These villains of the truth who ***cause*** and ***bring shame and dishonor*** on the possible ***VERY FEW LAWYERS*** who may be honest, ***should be brought to the fore, tarred and feathered in the public square, to be made an example of,*** for they are a ***disgrace*** to ***humanity.*** Because one ***goes to court*** to find **HONESTY,** only to come out ***disillusioned and disgusted*** with these possibly ***outrageous manipulators,*** who mete out those **BIASED** ***one-sided decisions!***

YES, finding your ***just cause*** in the ***court system*** which is filled with possible ***demoralization, erosion and prostitution*** of their souls is ***almost non-existent.*** They are sinking fast, downhill and ***each day*** they are getting **CLOSER TO THE DEVIL'S HELL. THIS IS A DECAYING STENCH THAT IS DETERIORATING IN EACH AND EVERY COURTROOM!**

Do you not sense the ***mutilation of the truth*** when you enter ***these unholy rooms? The poor flag standing innocently*** by the Judges Bench and at the mercy of somebody's whim **(not the truth.)** You can almost hear the voices of those in the shadows of our respected Flag.

How about the Judge apparently suppressing ***the good evidence*** you want to present? I know, yes, I have the honor whereby the Judge had possibly pre-determined the outcome before I was ever heard. Who knows **WHAT** ***juicy tid-bit*** was **WAIVED UNDER HIS NOSE OR HIS WALLET.**

In this case I am in presently, to my amazement, I have found ***something most unique.*** All the ladies in the courthouse have been so civil to me. They have been ***courteous and smile when they pass me in the hall,*** and perhaps one other gentleman. After all, I am ***an enemy to their system,*** as far as the adversaries are concerned. The lawyers for the other side are furious with me. I have held up this case for over three years-me as a **Pro-Se.**

I want ***the truth, the whole truth,*** which none of them want me to have. Even the ***Public Administrator*** who should possibly be ***neutral*** is on the ***other side.*** He will not talk to me: he has possibly lied on the witness stand to my questions and they were all covering up some **VERY BIG LIES!**

And this is another day in Surrogate Court for me. Yes, I am planning a book. I have already written some songs, **Lyrics, Music** and **Chords**. I wrote ***some twenty seven songs*** in 2 ½ weeks. I stopped at **27** because that is my **lucky** number. A week later, I wrote **14** more.

In one way I should thank them for this experience I am being put through, because if they had been ***honest*** and dealt with me ***judiciously,*** I may not be driven to write about the ***massacre*** **of the TRUTH!**

So something good has come out of this nightmare. This **holocaust** that I have been through in all these months-going back to Staten Island several times a month, trying to seek ***honesty***, **ha**! **IN THIS obviously contrived court system.**

IT IS TRULY A MIRACLE THAT I HAD TO PUT THIS EXPERIENCE DOWN ON PAPER, SO THAT YOU, MY DEAR READERS, WILL SEE YOU ARE NOT ALONE. I AM GRATEFUL THAT I TOOK

PEN IN HAND AND RELATED WHAT I HAVE BEEN THROUGH AT THE HANDS AND GAVEL OF THOSE BLACK ROBED JUDGES, WHO AT THEIR WHIM AND WHIMSY GIVE THEIR DECISIONS THAT ARE OBVIOISLY~~~~~~

BIASED…… TAINTED……..

DISHONEST…..AND

~~~~ FINALLY,

OUR PRAYERS WILL BE ANSWERED, AS WELL AS FOR THOSE WHO ARE AT THE MERCY OF THOSE MERCENARIES WHO ARE POSSIBLY RULED BY THEIR GREED AND THEIR NEED TO EMBELLISH THEIR FRIENDS. BECAUSE A GET RICH DECISION. WHICH

WILL DENY YOU OF YOUR JUST RIGHTS AND ENRICH THOSE WHO ARE NOT DESERVING, AND IN THE END……….

EVERYTHING EQUALS OUT!

BECAUSE OUR DEAR LORD

HAS <u>THE FINAL WORD! ~</u>

~~~ YOU WILL SEE!!!~~~

CHAPTER FOUR

"THE CORRUPTION IS BOUNTIFUL"

All I am seeking is ***justice*** in ***this case***, **and** if I have to open **PANDORA'S BOX** to bring out all ***the corruption, well so be it!!!***

The Judge has mystically shown his **true colors** in the **PUTNAM HEARING**, when the ***prime witness***, a friend who spent many, many days and evenings with the ***decedent*** who told him on various occasions, that he is an ***ALCOHOLIC, his complete testimony*** was **SUPPRESSED! IT WAS DELIBERATELY LEFT OUT OF THE REPORT! EVEN THE NAME OF THIS WITNESS,** who answered questions and related the incident and brought it out in the open, his name was ***wiped out.*** **SHOCKING! SHOCKING!**

So now I am totally convinced:

1) Who can **lie the best** and tell **the best lie,** and it does not matter if it is believable or not, as long as it serves **THEIR purpose.**

2) **If** you know the **Judge,** and he and **you have done business before, you have clear sailing!**

3) I rest my case with the Lord. If he has put me into this arena, I go with it. I am learning more about the ***common interest*** between **Judges and lawyers.**

While the court is ***also learning*** that a **Pro Se** can make ***a shambles*** out of their ***neatly contrived agenda***, I must put these notes down into a book. ***The public*** must know what I have been going through and that I, ***although I am not a lawyer,*** have to date, kept this case alive for over three years. If I had a lawyer, as the other side kept begging me constantly, **"GET A LAWYER,"** you know very well what would have happened. They would have flagrantly made their deals with him, and it would have been over in no time. But I cannot permit this apparent **crookedness** to **prevail,** so now we are going into about three years. **How about that…..**You know in other actions in the court system, I did have lawyers who **YES, SOLD ME OUT.** These darlings make their own deals. The ***client*** is only ***a vehicle*** for them. ***Without us they do not have a business!***

Is this not a sad commentary? When you go into court with a lawyer that you engage, he goes before a Judge, they now have a wedge to do **THEIR thing**. If the other side is possibly friendlier with the Judge, than your lawyer, then ***forget it!***

The ***deal*** apparently is in the bag in ***more ways than one.*** That is the way it is done, especially in a small town or borough. It is a ***closed shop*** . I know it, I've had it done to me, ***not once*** , ***not twice, not three times*** and now with this case, I am on my ***fourth outing.*** I already see the handwriting on the wall and the picture of what is happening as clear as a T.V. scenario.

Shall I say **'OH PITY ME,'** or shall I write about this new ***disgusting experience.*** This surrogate case could have been finished the very ***first day in court!*** It is now three years into this ***fiasco*** and the ***cover up*** is

rampant. My friend was taken ***advantage*** of on one of his ***binges. This lawyer/Will writer,*** **with** ***his wife and secretary,*** have done some very possible **ILLEGAL** things and the **COURT OBVIOUSLY KNOWS IT,** but they are all **'BROTHERS OF THE BLACK NIGHT,'** so they **are all hanging together** and they ***WILL*** **all hang together.**

The Judge is crushed because I want to have a ***jury.*** He, the Judge wants to try this case. Can you imagine the possible ***slaughtering*** the truth will take?

If I permit the ***culprits*** to possibly pull off this ***massive deception,*** I will never forgive myself. So this is what I believe:

1) If I see it thru and these ***corruptors*** win out, and if the Judge's final decision goes to the ***dishonest wrongful lawyers,*** with their forgeries and trickiness, then ***their*** **KARMA** ***and their families and loved ones*** fate will be sealed. They will not enjoy their **evil gains and games**. It will certainly **Boomerang** in the **most disastrous way.**

2) I now know for sure why I am in this case. Because ***they apparently are lying to me and also probably cheating me .*** They will all get what they ***deserve.*** They will ***not*** have ***any pleasure*** and they will ***not enjoy*** the bounty they have ***dishonestly*** taken from me. Just remember, the Lord ***cannot*** be set aside. Everything equals out. I understand fully well why I am in this venue. This is my purpose, for ***they who are probably cheating me, they***

will be punished, all of them. **EVERY ACT, GOOD OR BAD, DOES NOT GO UNHEEDED!**

So this is why I trust the decision from the Lord. He knows best how to deal with this ***deception, this fraudulence,*** circumvention of ***honesty*** **AND THE TRUTH.** And then I wonder…..***Is this possibly what is taught in the law schools?*** There does not seem to be any doubt. It seems to be ***so contagious***! Is it that he who could be the ***best liar*** in his class that makes ***the most vicious lawyer***? And then move on to the heights of this sick profession of **the Black Robed Brethren**? Why do these schools teach this ***type of law?*** A law that can be ***twisted*** and ***turned and manipulated*** so he can selfishly cut himself and his cohorts into all these ***nefarious deals*** that come before him?

So far I have had **four cases** before Judges and lawyers. Yes! four cases in the court system. The **DECISIONS, the COLLUSION, the PAYOFFS, the DISHONESTY. THERE IS NO HONOR AMONG THIEVES.**

Honesty seems to be forbidden in the courts. Your cases are only *a* ***vehicle*** or a ***greasing*** for the lawyers and Judges to possibly barter with. **YOUR CASE AND YOU ARE ONLY A PAWN IN THEIR HANDS.** The only concern they have is, ***" How do we split the spoils and the favors"?*** Also, how can they possibly get as many of their friends and relatives into this case?

And that is just what is going on in the courts. Last month I saw the ***very same lawyer*** come up with ***five cases*** in a row before the ***very same judge.*** I wonder what their split was???

~AND TO MAKE IT MORE UNPALATABLE, TO ADDRESS THESE MEN IN BLACK AS, "YOUR HONOR," BECAUSE WHEN YOU ENTER INTO A COURTHOUSE, THEY FRISK YOU AND YOUR POCKETS, POCKETBOOKS, BRIEFCASES ETC, IT IS MOST DEMEANING. THERE IS A DEGRADATION OF HONESTY. THE WHOLE SURROUNDING ATMOSPHERE SUGGESTS THE ODOR OF DEAL MAKING, DISREPECT FOR ALL HUMAN RIGHTS AND THE DEATH OF THE TRUTH, THAT PUNGENTLY PERMEATES THE ATMOSPHERE.

IT IS OVERWHELMING! IT IS THE EPITOME OF DISGUST. THE TEARS OF THOSE THAT HAVE BEEN CHEATED OF THEIR RIGHTS, RELYING ON THE POSSIBLE HONESTY OF THOSE ADDRESSED AS YOUR HONOR. IT COULD FILL OCEANS WITH THE TEARS OF THE MANY WHO HAVE SUFFERED AND LANGUISHED BECAUSE OF UNJUST DECISIONS AND I CAN VOUCH FOR THAT. THIS IS THE REASON THE ALMIGHTY GAVE ME THE FORTITUDE AND STRENGHT TO COME FORTH TO ENLIGHTEN YOU, MY DEAR READERS. HOW WELL I KNOW, BECAUSE OF MY EXPERIENCES AND BECAUSE THE MANY

OF MY FRIENDS WHO ARE BEING

CHEATED AND ROBBED AND MADE TO

SUFFER, FOR THOSE WHO DEEM IT

THEIR PREROGATIVE TO GET INTO

THAT UNHOLY BLACK ROBE.

THESE HONORED 'LEGALITES' ...

WALLOW IN IT'S

$$$$$$$$$$$$$$$$
$$$$$$$$$$$$$$$$

~~~~~**S T E N C H**~~~~~
~~~~~

CHAPTER FIVE

"CONSPIRACY"
"YOUR NAME IS JUDGE AND LAWYER"

When the sitting Judge told ***the lawyer/WILL Writer/Executor/attesting witness*** in conjunction with his ***wife***(in reality ***one person***); **"YOU BETTER GET A LAWYER,"** after he told the Judge he threw the **Power of Attorney** away-he took the Judge's advice and so-***that*** he did.

And as I told you earlier, the lawyer he got was none other but the ***Ex-Judge*** who sat on that ***very same bench*** for some **15+years**. I was in shock when the **Executive/WILL writer/lawyer/attesting witness** comes into court with his **'BIG GUN,'** to pull his ***chestnuts (of his own doing)*** out of the fire, you just know, something is ***very, very wrong!***

Dear friends, it just so happens that this **Ex-Judge,** ***now turned lawyer,*** whose picture still hangs high on the wall **(left of the bench)** in this same courtroom where he ***presided*** as a Judge ruling on cases that came before him, he ***still thinks he is possibly conducting business as usual,*** his ***ego*** will not let go! He still felt he was wearing that ***infamous robe*** bearing power, of the **'BLACK ROBE'**

So here we are now, ***this Ex-Judge*** is back in ***his*** courtroom, as a ***lawyer*** to defend ***this WILL WRITER CHARLATAN***; and who can do it better? He who sat in on all those past dealings and knew how to apparently ***circumvent the truth!***

But now, of course, without the **Black Robe Camouflage** to give him the false security that automatically goes along when they ***don*** that **Black Mantel,** he obviously still thinks he is the one in charge.

Well ***this Ex-Judge, now turned lawyer*** for this ***WILL MAKER LIAR*** was truly something else. So, when he finished questioning ***his well prepared witnesses*** it **WAS MY TURN TO TAKE OVER AND QUESTION THEM.**

Well they took the **oath**, over the **Bible** with **the American Flag** behind them, and while **the Judge** sat on the Bench, I prepared to ask the questions.

This **Ex-Judge/lawyer** for this **WILL WRITER** had obviously coached his clients so well, they all memorized their ***lies*** and ***lines*** to the **"T."** He practically ***nudged*** the ***falsehoods*** out of ***their lying mouths*** with such ***facility,*** I could not help but think, it was a **Broadway show** I ***was sadly witnessing.***

Now that it was ***my turn to question his clients,*** he **JUMPED AT EVERY CHANCE TO OBJECT TO MY QUESTIONS WHILE THE LIES WERE FLYING FAST AND FURIOUS.** Believe me, it was ***a show not to be missed***. And dear friends, **THIS WAS NOT A DRESS REHEARSAL,** by any means. ***This, was the real thing!!***

MY witnesses were ***not rehearsed.*** **They did not have to be. They were telling the truth.** My manager who spent **every weekend** with our **deceased friend** took the witness stand. I questioned him, again I say, **'unrehearsed'**. He said the deceased party voluntarily admitted to us that he was ***an Alcoholic, who attended the AA meetings*** and had recorded tapes for sale to the public about **ALCOHOLISM**, with the **Great D'ARTEGA** and his **Orchestra** for the background music.

Well, ***shock of all shocks***.....you simply must read the decision that the ***sitting Judge*** apparently put ***his name*** to. I am positive that ***the Ex-Judge*** drew up this ***pack of lies*** and the Judge on the bench conspicuously ***signed it.***

This **Putnam Hearing** was filled with such possibly *sick* ***falsehoods,*** there was no doubt who composed this disaster. Yet ***the Judge*** on the Bench ***signed it.*** How could he put his name to this ***fraudulently written report?***

When my business manager finished my questioning, telling about the decedents visits and conversations, and ***that he was an*** **ALCOHOLIC,** and ***because of us he stopped his drinking and smoking,*** the Judge commended him saying-**"YOU WERE THE BEST WITNESS HERE TODAY."**

Then ***why oh why,*** was his testimony, his name and the answers he gave ***totally cancelled and obliterated*** from the final report of the important ***Putnam Hearing?*** It was as if he was **NEVER THERE!!!**

So you can see the apparent ***power*** of ***this Ex-Judge/ turned lawyer,*** had a difficult time giving up that **filthy Black Robe**, which gave those who wear it, **Carte Blanche** to run ***rough-shod*** over the ***truth!***

I was truly sick. I did not want to believe that the ***sitting Judge*** could possibly put ***his signature*** to this piece of **TRASH!** And ***the lies*** apparently written by ***his predecessor.***

Well to my amazement and I do mean ***amazement***, the next time we came to court, and I looked up at the wall where this Ex-Judge's picture hung all those years, **IT WAS GONE!** Gone from the right side of the wall in that courtroom and **SO, WAS THE EX-JUDGE**. He suddenly ***walked out of the case.*** I am sorry to have to laugh, but somehow I see in my mind that he took his ***dusty likeness*** from the wall, put it under his arm and left. **HE QUIT!!!**

To further the mystery of the disappearing **Ex-Judge** and **his picture**, it appears from the ***whispers*** in the court that he asked his client for more money and this alleged ***WILL/writer/lawyer*** refused him.

DEAR FRIENDS, IS THIS NOT THE EPITOME OF INTRUGUE? OH, MYSTERY OF MYSTERIES, WHAT GOES ON UNDER THEIR BLACK ROBES? THE CHICANERY,... THE GAMES, ...THE PLOTTINGS, ... THE DEAL MAKING,... THE DISHONESTY,... THE CHEATING,...THE FALSIFICATIONS,... THE CRAFTINESS,... THE

CONCEALMENTS, …THE SUBTERFUGE,…

THE SIN COMMITTING,…THE

TRANGRESSIONS,… AND FINALLY…..

THE CORRUPTIONS, ….. THAT LEAD TO

THESE NEFARIOUSLY, SHAMEFUL,

SCANDALOUS, DIABOLICALY, SINFUL

ACTS ~~~~~~~

AND TO POSSIBLY DISHONOUR THE

LAW, WITH THESE INSIDIOUSLY,

DISGUSTING, SINFUL ACTS, IN THE NAME OF

JUSTICE.

~~~~~~~AND SO I SAY~~~~-~~

"CONSPIRACY"

YOUR NAME IS JUDGE AND LAWYER!!!

CHAPTER-SIX

"DECEIVE, DELAY AND DESTROY"

Deceive, Delay and Destroy, what a title for a song-but sadly enough, it is the ***reality*** in our **court system.** For ***that*** is apparently what happens within those walls when ***a sitting Judge allows, permits and condones justice*** to probably be ***massacred*** at the hands of a ***probably dishonest*** ***Executive/Lawyer*** who has taken for granted the law into ***his own dirty little hands,*** because the Judge obviously lets him get away with it even though I have ***constantly brought this topic to the fore.***

How do I know this? Well, it **IS**, and **HAS** happened to me ***not once, not twice, not three times*** but this is the ***fourth time*** that I have the displeasure of trying to find ***the 'elusive,' (you should excuse me), justice!*** It is for this reason, I have refused to have ***any lawyer, high priced*** by their own ***egotistical, over-rated value,*** to handle my law cases.

This new subterfuge I am living through in this present law case, where I am **Pro Se,** in the Surrogate Court, is proof positive of the ***prevailing dishonesty*** that conspicuously ***does persist*** in the ***dishonorable and disgusting court system. A system running wild, and unchecked with corruption and no constraints to the written law,*** with **JUDGES POLICING THEMSELVES,** and their comrades.~ And only in ***our beautiful America ~ can they get away with this lawlessness.***

So I say, I am sorry for the person who has to go into a court to find the ***justice*** in a matter that ***might rightfully be his,*** only to find that he is obviously **BEING USED** by the ***lawyer as a tool*** whose only interest is **his fees**. He is then possibly **manipulated** for the ***benefit of both the lawyer and the Judge,*** while this poor unsuspecting soul gets lost in ***their dubious swindle.*** That is why I prefer being **Pro Se.** At least **THIS WAY**, I know what is going on without being a pawn in the hands of these **'SHARKS.'**

Now you can see how this all works:

1. **IF** I engage a lawyer-they can then meet in the Judge's chambers-***Would the Judge ever meet with me?***

2. **IF** I engage a lawyer-they can make their possible secret deals-***Would the Judge make any kind of deal with me?***

3. **If** I engage a lawyer-they can have dinners together– ***Would the Judge ever have dinner with me?***

4. **If** I engage a lawyer-they can pass party favors with each other – ***Would, and could he do that with me?***

5. If I engage a lawyer- ***Would I have Carte Blanche to call the Judge and speak with him whenever, as these so called Barristers have privilege to? ETC, ETC…..***

6. This is one miserable mess – it is totally out of hand. In fact, I know someone who had engaged a lawyer and ***when this lawyer found out that his client*** was almost out of monies, he said to him ***"You had better get another attorney, this is as far as I go."***

IT IS TRULY A SAD DAY FOR ALL PEOPLE CONCERNED, THAT WE HAVE TO RELY ON LAWYERS AND JUDGES FOR A SOLUTION, ONLY TO BE MET AT TIMES, WITH DISAPPOINTMENT AND HEARTBREAK.

ARE THESE JURISTS NOT FEARFUL THAT THEY TAKE IT UPON THEMSELVES TO PLAY GOD AND DISPOSE OF YOUR CASE, BY POSSIBLY HOW MUCH THE GOING PRICE IS THAT DAY?

WHY DO NOT THE SCHOOLS OF HIGHER LEARNING MAKE IT MANDATORY TO INCLUDE SEVERAL SEMESTERS ON BEING ABOVE THE TEMPTATION OF BRIBERY. PERHAPS A COURSE ON THE EVIL LURES FOR PERSONAL GREED AND THE SHAME OF THESE ETERNAL SINS THAT CLING TO YOUR LIFE AS IT GROWS WITH EACH INSURECTION.

THERE IS NO GOOD DEED THAT COULD EVER UNDO THE HARM IT DOES TO POSSIBLY ACCEPT GIFTS AND MONIES TO PLACE YOUR GAVEL OF APPORVAL ON A TAINTED, MONEY BOUGHT DECISION….. AND YET WE WAIT FOR AN HONEST CULMINATION TO THE PROBLEM WHICH HAS ALREADY BEEN DETERMINED BEHIND THOSE CLOSED CHAMBER'S DOORS.

SO BE IT!!

CHAPTER-SEVEN

"THE EVER ELLUSIVE JUSTICE"

For an ***honest person*** to find ***justice*** in any courtroom is almost ***next to impossible.*** Unless, you have been lucky enough to slip through the cracks or to ***know*** some of the ' **BAG MEN,**' for most of the ***Judges.*** **THIS** is what I have found in those hideous malfeasance law ***un-abiding*** buildings. The ***motto*** is: ***'You have to have the right intro and the right connections!"***

I know I have had lawyers who ***practice*** on **BOTH SIDES** of the scale. They took **MY** good monies and in conjunction with ***favors*** from the **'OTHER SIDE.'**

They knew the ropes, (which many times would do much better around ***their necks and their pocket books.)***

It is a game – ***not*** of chance, by no means, ***but*** if you know the **'SHAMAS' (the Judge's bag man) you have got it made!**

And so it goes, ***through*** the ages that is what this ***whole stinking mess*** is about.

And this, you the public, do not in any way realize that, we put these **BLACK ROBED BANDITS** in ***business.*** Remember, before they became a Judge, they were **a struggling lawyer,** ***an ambulance chaser!*** But, with the right ***political connection,*** **AND ABOUT $50,000,** they now wear the **'BLACK ROBE'** and **voila,** not to be **outdone** – he thinks he is **GOD**!

Well, now the picture changes. Instead of the Judge looking for favors, these lawyers and such, come to ***his highness,*** come to ***his throne*** bringing all types of ***deals, goodies and favors,*** to get in with ***this man*** in the

BLACK ROBE. They are looking to get a ***favorable decision.*** **HE…..IS NOW A RECEIVER.**

Now, ***ponder*** this – once he becomes a ***Judge*** there are **NO EXPENSES.** They get the ***electric free, no*** bills for **RENTING THAT BENCH, (*if only that wooden bench that some tree that hosted beautiful birds, sheltered you in the rain, had to be cut down to make this seat* for *his 'low ness,'*)** so for him to make a business ***for himself and his cronies,*** he has not a penny to pay. ***No expenses*……*only profits*…….**He is **NOW** in business for himself, a most **LUCRATIVE** position, and he acquires this ***haughty deceptive attitude.*** Then, possible breach of promise to the ***oath*** they took and their double dealings. It is such a ***disgrace*** and so ***dishonorable,*** **AND YET WE obviously PAY** their ***sleazy disgusting salaries*** while they are collecting the **BIG BUCKS** and **FAVORS** from their friends, in addition.

Yes, they sure have it made. No questions asked, and they must be addressed as, **"YOUR HONOR."** So you see how you become a pawn in the hands of **some** of ***these ogres.***

Remember, they need ***your cases*** so they can possibly do ***their bartering*** with your ***lawyer*** or whoever else is of interest. Without your case, they have a **'Dry Well'**. But the minute you engage one of the ***'Attache-carrying cut throats,'*** the action begins. By that I mean these **BLACK ROBED DEMONS** in human shapes, ***start not* YOUR *action, but* THEIR *action.***

Now the lawyers; how do they make a connection with the Judge or how can he be ***reached,*** who is his **SHAMAS?** How can a ***deal*** be made?

I remember in an action I had a while ago where we paid ***these wretched scum*** of the earth ***(our lawyers)*** lots of money to help get ***justice*** in ***an anti-trust case.*** They would have lunch with the ***adversary lawyers,*** then come back and sit with us. They would go ***arm in arm*** to the restaurant, then sit with them at the same table and ***joke and cajole*** in ***camaraderie*** and pretend to solicit the law for us. They even made calls to me from the ***adversary offices*** asking me pertinent questions ***(can you imagine that?)*** So, my engaged lawyers were getting it from **BOTH SIDES!**

This is just a ***sampling*** of what has happened to me. I am ***justified*** in not trusting some of them connected to the court business or any phase of it.

Now in **Joseph Borkin's** book ***"The Corrupt Judge,"*** published by Clarkson N. Potter, it is an exhaustive and authoritative account of such ***judicial corruption***, it will ***shock you!*** In his book he has intensified case histories of Judges and lawyers, shocking as it is, one of the gilt edge law firms that was one of the lawyers for my adversary awhile back.

Well, ***that firm*** paid a Judge ***$250,000*** to have a case thrown out, so in turn, that Judge gave them the ***favorable decision they wanted.*** Yes, on the inside flap he mentions this ***particular case,*** that the ***Judge*** was ***bribed*** for. He had his car parked down the street from the courthouse.

He scans the "Entire history of ***misconduct*** in the ***United States Federal Judiciary.*** The ***bribes*** ranged for jobs for ***Judge's sons,*** to ***payments*** in some cases, to awarding ***multi-million dollar*** steel plant deals." Giving credit to Mr. Borkins's book, ***Decisions*** were ***sold*** for (get this) ***cash loans, favors, business opportunities.*** As he said in the book, the ***pay-offs*** took place in the back ***alleys and judicial chambers.*** For every ***corruptible Judge,*** there are ***inevitable corruptors.***

So, when you bring a case into this ***whore house, (I mean court house),*** it is worse than going to a race track , at least at the race track you can see the horse you put your bucks on run, but in the legal business it is all plotted out in those, **'Clandestine meetings.'** Then they all show up in the courtroom with the Judge in his **UNHOLY BLACK ROBE** to re-enact the scene as **REHEARSED IN THEIR PRIVACY**.

I recall the chief Judge in a case I had for **ANTI-TRUST,** his **'BAG-MAN,'** was always trying to placate me. His actual words to me in the hall **(my dear mother was present too, she always accompanied me to court),** he would say to us , "***God does not put more on your shoulders than you can carry.***"

I'll tell you this, he sure could carry that load that my adversaries gifted that Judge with. By the way, this Judge was originally ***a lawyer*** in ***one of these gilt edged law firms*** and his ***'bag man,'*** never left his side. He was well aware of the deals those lawyers made with his buddy- **'THE JUDGE!'** Did I forget to mention, when we would meet as we were about to enter the Judge's chambers, you could not stand ***his breath.*** **(How could he booze up so early in the morning?)**

After the first day in court, with me acting as ***Pro Se***, the sessions thereafter were held in ***privacy in the CHIEF JUDGE'S private chambers.*** They did not want the public to obviously see what they were pulling off, with ***His highness*** seated at the head of this long ***un-legal table.***

I was seated at his left, and my publisher/manager was beside me. Opposite were ***my adversaries***, **SIX LIARS (LAWYERS,)** from the biggest law firms in this country, and of course, ***they were the Judge's friends!'*** You would be stunned if you knew the firms they represented against ***little me.*** And all I wanted was ***justice*** as an ***American Plaintiff.*** But to think, the high powered ***influentially engaged*** against me, to thwart my case.

The reason that I had becom***e Pro Se*** was: my first lawyers, who were **supposed** to be our friends, were taken care of by the ***other side.*** To drop our case, they were given ***a swimming pool, a trip to Europe, and $50,000.00 retainer*** for another clients case, that ***wetted*** their ***avaricious appetites,*** after ***we were paying them*** good monies. They first had a tacit agreement, ***NOT*** to ***push my case***, then they dropped out without telling me my day in court was coming up. So I had ***to post a very large bond*** to get my Action back in on the docket. ***Crooks,*** yes that is what these ***supposed lawyer friends*** did to us.

That is why the chief Judge and the adversary lawyers had my case heard only in the ***Judge's private chambers.*** It must never be ***seen or heard*** in the ***open courtroom,*** especially with me as a ***Pro Se.*** I tell you, it was sickening the way they, my adversaries, would write the decisions for all the motions and that ***well greased Judge,*** would obviously sign his ***dishonorable name*** to their papers **(when you read the wording , you just knew it.)** And, the Judge's decision was ***so biased,*** the way it was worded, it was just so obvious as to who wrote it. It was blatantly written by those '***gilt edged law firms'*** and of course friends of **(you know who),** the **'BLACK ROBED ONE!'**

Yes, it was too dangerous for a ***Pro Se*** such as me , to be in the ***open court*** for the public ***to witness*** what was going on. They did not wish to have this in the court, out in the open, for all to see how **JUSTICE** was ***being thwarted!*** ~Again, all I wanted was ***the truth and justice.*** But is it not a travesty? For these **benched ones** to play **God,** with others who only want ***honesty and justice?***

When I went home every night from this ***nightmare of lies***, ***deals and the slaughtering of the truth,*** I prayed that the justice I was seeking in this corrupt court system would see the light of day.

It was ***a sick, sick scene.*** They were ***getting richer.*** I was ***getting wiser.*** And, the court reporter thanked me for getting him richer because of my case ***in this Federal Court.*** They were all happy as long as this action kept on, because their billings and the deal makings were being kept alive in a **BIG WAY!!!!**

And now I prayed to our Lord to help, and this is how **KARMA** works. Today, not one of these honorable law firm Judges involved in thwarting the truth in this court are ***no longer here.*** Today, they are probably being ***rewarded*** by ***the*** **DEVIL,** for the great job they did. The torture they put me through with ***their lies,*** and their writing of the Judges decision with the Judge affixing **HIS** name to their documents, were ***biased and crooked.***

Believe me that was a **very *important big case.*** I will not mention the law firms involved, it would shock you to know who ***these crooks*** are with their power. Can you imagine the ***gifts and favors*** that transpired in order to keep ***my case private and awa***y from the ***OPEN COURT*** into the ***Judges chambers*** for the public not to see , ….a ***Pro Se*** trying to get justice?

There **is no honor among thieves,** I can say. And so, this is why I am writing about it. I have gotten one way biased treatment ***four times*** in our great court system.

My cases were ***all fabulous-all four of them.*** And, this will one day, make a shocking movie. The names involved would stun you. The Judges were originally lawyers in these **gilt edged law firms** that were opposite me. So, what chance did I have of getting ***an honest decision?***

Now, the worst thing that can happen to a Judge is to deal with a **Pro Se.** ***They are furious.*** They cannot ***make a deal with me.*** They ***cannot pull a swindle job their way,*** and sadly they cannot help their friends and cohorts. ***I'm in their way.***

IN THIS CASE NOW, the Judge repeatedly says **"GET A LAWYER, GET A LAWYER!" "BUT I WILL NOT AND I DID NOT!!"** I am holding back the settling of the **ESTATE** of my friend. There are **THREE WILLS.** The last two written ***ten days apart and corrupt by the lawyer.*** I will not sign this ***deceptive lie.***

There is much ***suppression of the truth*** by all the ***witnesses. Perjury and dishonest tactics*** and yes, ***the prevarication and evasions,*** also, the Judge on the bench is dubiously ***aiding*** and ***abetting*** this ***film flam.*** This is an experience **I MUST WRITE ABOUT.** The Ex-Judge ***and*** the one in his **Black Robe** on the bench, ***are***

conspicuously distorting the honesty in **this case.** ***All in that court house knew*** **EXACTLY** ***what is going on. They are camouflaging honesty.*** After all, I am a **Pro Se** seeking ***the truth.*** In their minds, I had ***no business wanting the truth*** in their private court on Staten Island – **THAT SMALLEST BOROUGH with possibly the BIGGEST LIES**– and **cover ups,** while they make their own laws in order ***to benefit themselves.***

Yes. Little me, like **DAVID** and **GOLIATH,** I only want what is ***proper and right.*** But that is not how this court works. The **DISHONESTY REEKS** the moment you enter that ***infamous building.*** And then the courtroom, with its ***ominous bench*** waiting to seat the Judge who may have already prepared ***his decision*** in ***his chambers.***

Strangely enough I keep thinking, I live in a beautiful world surrounded with beautiful sounds, ***all natures colorful birds*** that serenade me daily in my back yard and in front of my home with heavenly melodies that our dear Lord, miraculously bestowed upon them. Then of course all ***the instruments I play*** and create my beautiful ***songs*** and ***loving lyrics*** with natures harmonies.

Yes, I am surrounded with all this gentleness and beauty and then for a brief moment, a thought suddenly enters my mind of the **EVIL** ***vibrations*** in ***that court*** and all that you and ***your families will suffer possibly***, and how the salaries you make with ***those devious intrigues,*** and all the **HARM** you are doing to ***your souls.*** And the **KARMA** you are creating is ***so cruel,*** and you are doing it all ***by yourselves.*** Yes, the minute you enter ***that manufacturing plant,*** your ***castle of*** **CORRUPTION, THAT THREE RING FARCE (without the**

kangaroos) where **the CORONER IN HIS BLACK REGALIA,** is ready to bury the **FACTS and the TRUTHS. The *whole scene, those benches,*** the witness chairs and all **THE PUTRID STENCH** of decisions possibly embroidered with **THE SEAL OF ONE'S INFAMY.**

The contrast of my lifestyle, and that of **THOSE** who work in the courthouse, is one that is **truly amazing.**

What you sow, **SO SHALL YE REAP!** Have you ever seen a Ferris Wheel? One moment the seat is ***on top,*** the next it is ***on the bottom***. **AND SO IT IS. *What goes up*** MUST ***come down!***

As for **YOU who RECONSTRUCT *the law*** to **FIT YOUR POCKETBOOKS** and fill your **AVARICIOUS APPETITES……..**the **THUD** is so great when you **SCRAPE THE** BOTTOM**.**

THAT, …… IS YOUR DESTINY FOR

PLAYING GOD ……WITH OTHER PEOPLES'

LIVES AND THEIR CASES. …….

……..AND GOD WILL NOT BE SET ASIDE…….

ESPECIALLY FOR YOU,….

WHO THINK…………

YOU ARE…….

GOD!

AND HAVE TAKEN IT UPON YOURSELF TO ACT IT OUT WITH GAVEL IN HAND…..OR SHOULD I SAY:

"HAVE GAVEL WILL TRAVEL."

CHAPTER EIGHT

"THE GREAT COVER UP-OR THE DEALS UNDER THE BLACK ROBES"

No, no I cannot let this go by. What I am going through in that Surrogate's Court, is truly ***abominable!*** The possible ***robbery,*** the ***thievery,*** the ***lie telling,*** the ***cover-ups, the engaging of*** the Ex-Judge who ***plowed that court*** for some ***fifteen years,*** coming back now ***as a lawyer,*** with his picture that hung on the wall in **THAT** courtroom!

The integrity of the silence that emanates from that **EVIL** ***place*** in that possibly ***God forsaken Borough,*** left ***a message of great importance*** for me and so here it is:

My job is done here and now. And so, I did my best for you to perhaps see **WHO** and **WHAT** I am. How you; ***each and everyone of you***, treated me. ***Your conduct, your avaricious lies, your disrespect for the truth*** and ***your manipulations***...**SAD, SAD!!**

You have all apparently **earned** and ***registered your conduct*** in **your KARMIC calendar.** You each have earned what you and yours will get and receive. You ***can fight amongst each other, blame each other*** here on this **SICK LITTLE ISLAND**, ***in this musty secret ridden building*** where the truth is put to **'DEATH DAILY.'** ***(the Court House.)***

I want no part of this type of ***legal maneuverings*** that is practiced in secrecy here. I have ***learned a great lesson how greed and dishonesty can eat into your souls,*** and I know now what you all have conspicuously done to me ***with your plotting to take away what is rightfully mine.***

I am grateful that the part I played in **D'ARTEGA** and **BERNARD'S** life was ***a healthy wholesome one.*** I can truthfully say I am doing the Lord's work here as I do all my life, with people and animals.

What can YOU say? Take a pen and paper and try to write ***all the things you did to me in this court case.*** Ask yourselves, "**Did you do what was right? Was I honest to that Lady?**" Your answer should shock you **IF,** you were honest with your reply, you will then know your fate! ***Your* EVILNESS** to me, ***will all come back to you* AND *your loved ones.***

Your conduct ***(all of you)*** proved one positive thing for me, because you all seem to work with the **DEVIL**, whereas **I** work with **GOD**. You will never ***wash this sin off your soul.*** I could see all the **trumped up deals, YOU AND THE JUDGE OBVIOUSLY CREATED.** You all played your parts well. I saw through it all, and **SO** did the Lord.

Do you not have ***any shame*** for your ***disgusting conduct?*** It certainly is a ***sad reflection*** of your possible ***upbringing and your background***. The saying is, **"THE APPLE DOES NOT FALL FAR FROM THE TREE!"** What I was a witness to for those ***three years*** in ***THAT courthouse,*** leads me to believe this ***adage,*** but I wonder, **WHAT** ***tree*** could **YOU possibly** refer to?

Well, enough said, ***our lifestyles*** are totally different. You can have **THIS SICK COURT SCENE,** day in and day out undoubtedly ***filled with lies and cheating.*** I will do my music and bring joy and happiness to all my audiences. So we are through. Our worlds are miles apart, ***literally and figuratively.***

~AND, THE LORD,...WILL DO HIS THING....BECAUSE OF ALL THE PAIN AND AGONY THAT YOU HAVE APPARENTLY CAUSED SO MANY PEOPLE THAT HAVE TRUSTED AND BELIEVED IN YOU, AND HOPED AND PRAYED FOR YOUR JUST AND HONEST DECISIONS.

LET IT NOT BE SAID THAT WE GO TO COURT AND ARE VICTIMIZED BY THOSE WHO HAVE THE POWER TO HEAL OUR SUFFERING AND SOLVE OUR PROBLEMS.

FOR IS THAT NOT THE JOB OF THE JUDICIARY, INSTEAD OF CREATING MORE HAVOC FOR THE JUST AND DESERVING?

WE LOOK UP TO THESE ROBED ONES FOR A SALVATION AND TOO MANY TIMES COME OUT DEJECTED AND CRESTFALLEN, WITH THEIR SUPPOSEDLY BIASED DECISION. HOW DOES IT MAKE THEM FEEL TO BETRAY AND DENY SO MANY OF US OF OUR RIGHTFUL DECISIONS.

DO NOT THESE PEOPLE HAVE A CONSCIENCE? ARE THEY EVER HAUNTED BY THE EXPRESSIONS ON THOSE FACES THAT THEY SO BLATANTLY DENIED JUSTICE TO?

AS THEY DRIVE HOME, DO THEY TAKE THE PICTURE OF THOSE PEOPLE THEY HAVE TRAMPLED ON IN THEIR COURTROOM, THAT IS PROBABLY SO FILLED WITH SORROW AND DISTORTION?

WHICH SOMETIMES

SOME OF US

REGRETTABLY

GOT AND HAD TO LIVE

WITH,

BECAUSE OF THEIR POSSIBLE MONEY-BOUGHT DECISION.

CHAPTER-NINE

"IN MY EXPERIENCE"

In my experience, I find the ***judiciary*** is worse than **MAFIA**. At least **MAFIA** can be put in jail.

But, the **CULPRITS** in the *judiciary* cannot be put in jail, because they cover their tracks, at least the ones I've had the ***displeasure of dealing with,*** as a plaintiff in ***several cases.***

I say this because of my experiences with ***lawyers and Judges,*** with them and their ***unlawful discretions.***

~And so I feel most confident that the Lord is keeping score of these **BLACK ROBED SATANS~**

Honesty is conspicuously not part of their ***'deal making.'*** They have **'Carte *Blanche' to steal, to mete out their biased decisions, to return favors to their friends and families or whatever pleasure they care to partake of.*** That is the way this game is played.

I know only too well, because they have **DONE IT TO ME** and they **WILL DO IT TO YOU..** And, you can be sure their **KARMA** will confront them for their acts and it will **ALL EVEN OUT.**

Yes, I have seen it. It always has evened out in the past, and they ***(these evil ones-the Judges and lawyers)*** and their loved ones will have to pay God's way for what they have **DONE** and are **DOING** to me through the years.

Why do you think I have been brought into the paths of these ***possibly corruptible legal tenders;*** because they needed to be **judged** and ***evaluated*** for their ***lies and mistreatments*** that they have afforded me.

I do not have an enemy in all this world. Whoever has wronged me in the past, their **KARMA** has dealt completely with them for all their misdoings to me. I am ***most confident*** because I have seen it happen!

However, of one thing I am sure, **I, AS A PLAINTIFF WITH TWO CASES WHERE MY LAWYERS WERE WELL PAID, AND MY TWO CASES, AS A PLAINTIFF PRO SE,** getting ***justice*** in the ***United States court system*** is **NEXT** to **IMPOSSIBLE**, unless you are a ***benefactor*** in any of many ways. ~And yet, I know for every ***misdeed*** someone has done to me, in some way I've been delightfully rewarded, and to those who have perpetrated their ***dishonesty***, they have paid, whether themselves or a loved one, for their sins to **ME.** You cannot have someone spill tears for something you have caused them, without it possibly coming ***back to you!***

~And strangely enough, they who have wronged me have apparently brought about this ***plague*** by themselves. **THAT, IS KARMA!**....

And you ***may wonder,*** and you ***may ask***, "How come you were inspired to write ***these words, these songs,*** **these** ***poems*** about the ***judiciary system in America?***

Well, when this book is published and during any interviews, I will spell out the ***whole stinking mess*** that I have lived with, and had to put up with, in this ***ungodly sick legal system.*** A system that apparently condones ***your own lawyers*** being paid off by ***your adversaries*** to throw my cases, and ***Judges who supposedly have EX-PARTE meetings*** **without me.**

In fact, when my attorneys were busy underhandedly handling my case, they were also, at the very same time, busy doing a possible hatchet job, on **CARVEL** and **VOLKSWAGEN,** ***two of their clients.***

~And, finally, when the **Federal Agents** were closing in on them, and the N.Y. TIMES wrote the story about what **THEY** did in those ***two cases,*** I received a phone call from that **CROOKED LAWYER** that ***very day*** asking to speak to **MY PUBLISHER!!**

I said, after what you characters did to us, we do not ever want to speak with you ***again.*** Then this **MISERABLE SELLOUT LAWYER** said, "We must leave the country **TODAY**, - in fact we are at the airport **NOW.** We are on our way to **Puerto Rico.** If you have today's NewYork Times, you will see ***the story on the front page.*** We are ***truly sorry*** for what we did to you. ***The Federal Agents are after us."***

Well, I never heard from them again! I feel quite sure that their **KARMA** has been met…And so it will be:

WHOEVER HAS DONE SOMETHING VERY WRONG TO ME. YES THEY WILL PAY

GOD'S WAY…..

AND ONE MORE THING…..

'THERE IS NO APPEALING…..

GOD'S DECISION.!!

CHAPTER-TEN

"IT IS A GAME~THOUGH SADLY"

When I awakened this morning, it was very clear to me. I had found the **'SOLUTION.'** Yes, I now know how ***this whole*** **un-legalized/legal business** works. You must hear what I discovered.

Being a well trained musician from the tender age of three and one half, I now, at this time, discovered how the American Courts ***operate.*** As a musician playing several instruments, composing, and conducting when I see **a 'B' flat note,** you can only play **a 'B' flat note,** not a **'D' flat or a 'G' flat or a flatted 9th. , but only a 'B' flat note** and **"THAT IS THAT!"** It is universal, yes music is a universal language, and that holds through the ages!

But, and this is surely a big **'BUT'** in the court system, we have a very different situation. It is a business alright and under cover. There, it is called **INTERPRETATION!**

So, they can possibly take **a 'B' note** and they can **twist** and **turn** it and they ***manipulate it*** so that it no longer sounds like ***a 'B' note.*** And, that allows some of these Judges to perhaps interpret the laws **TO FIT** their ***deep pockets*** and ***situations!***

Can you imagine what the great composers like **Mozart, Liszt** or **Bach** would have sounded like if the great Opera's were left for lawyers and Judges to interpret? Why, ***the notes*** in their music would sound like ***a catastrophe.*** They would ***mutilate*** their scores as **THEY ONLY TOO WELL KNOW HOW**! And furthermore, it would be ***totally unrecognizable!*** That is **EXACTLY** what is happening in **OUR COURT SYSTEM TODAY!**.....

Yes, the guise of **MANIPULATION** and **INTERPRETATION** of the **LAW,** is the problem. Thank GOD, these **miserable jurists** are **NOT MUSICAL PERFORMERS AND WRITERS**, otherwise we possibly would have ***a*** **HODGEPODGE, a CACOPHONY** ***of*** **DISHARMONIES** the likes of which you have **NEVER HEARD**. They, ***these lawyers*** and ***these Judges*** have the happy proclivity of ***manipulating words, thoughts, laws,*** and whatever they get their ***tight fisted little hands*** into, and the only time they open them is ...**....YOU KNOW WHEN!!!!**

No one has the right to interpret or to change the laws for their convenience, no more than taking Beethoven and souping it up with their own ***disharmonious notes.*** So why go to school to study the laws? They do not abide by them. They are always and forever making their own ***laws and rules,*** and how well I know, **OH YES,** with my experiences in several courts seeking this **'MAN MADE JUSTICE.'**

Do these **BLACK ROBES possibly** have ***Carte Blanche*** in the courtrooms of our America to ***Massacre,*** to **Mutilate** the laws that were handed down? By the way, all those hundreds of books on the shelves in law offices; ***never, never*** is one ***out of place. Those books,*** they are ***a subterfuge,*** it gives them the credibility to ask for their ***handsome fees.*** Tell me, do they ever open them? Possibly only to see how they can ***twist*** or ***turn*** the words on those pages to ***fit their wallets.*** And so, these people who play with **Your Lives, Your Souls** –

they ***sit and Judge,*** and take ***our cases*** and have their ***way,*** while they figure out how to **sock it to you,** and all those poor people who come to them for their great, '**Solomonistic' decree,** as **a** ***solution*** to their problems.

OH SHAME OF SHAMES... PITY OF ALL PITIES,.... AND JURIST OF ALL JURISTS, ...THY NAME IS .....

'YOUR HONOR???

AND A PRO SE,.... SHALL TEACH THEM .....

~ 'HONESTY.'~

TAKING ON THE POSITION OF BEING A PRO SE IN ANY COURT, IS A VERY DIFFICULT UNDERTAKING. IT IS A DEMEANING AND THORNY TASK. YOU ARE HATED AND OSTRICIZED BY THE LAWYERS AND THE JUDGE, BECAUSE YOU ARE HINDERING THEM FROM DOING THEIR THING.

IN MY EXPERIENCE, AS A PRO SE, IN ALL MY CASES, AS A PLAINTIFF, (two cases with attorneys and two cases as a Pro Se) I WAS UNFOURTUNATELY SOLD OUT BY MY LAWYERS, AND POSSIBLY THEIR COMPATRIOT, THE JUDGE!

IS THE SUBJECT OF HONESTY

ELABORATED ON, IN THOSE LEGAL BOOKS, (besides gathering dust on the shelves.) ARE THEY EVER REMOVED TO LOOK UP SOME LAW TERMINOLOGY THAT COULD POSSIBLY BENEFIT A LEGAL CASE?

WHEN WE ENGAGE A LAWYER AND WE GO TO COURT, WE EXPECT AN HONEST VERDICT. WE DO NOT PAY OUR LAWYERS GOOD MONIES TO BE VICTIMIZED BY THE JUDGE FOR A PROBABLY FALSE AND BIASED DECISION WHICH IS A TOTAL DISGRACE AND MOST UN-BEFITTING FOR SOMEONE WHO IS ADDRESSED AS……

'YOUR HONOR.'

CHAPTER ELEVEN

"THE PURVEYERS OF JUSTICE WHO HAVE MUTILATED AND CONTAMINATED THE LAW AS IT IS"

Now if someone were to ask me what my opinion is of this ***Court System,*** in our country, I would not hesitate to answer-***"It is possibly a business,* WITH** and **FOR** ***the Judges*** and ***the lawyers,*** and their **"Bag *Men,"*** who ***front and collect for them."***

In other words, it is a ***wheeling dealing*** set up. I have had four actions as a plaintiff in this apparently ***dishonorable profession of Judges and lawyers.*** They, are ***Hucksters, Barterers, Backstabbers, Dealmakers, Crooks*** and any other **POSSIBLE** ***vile name*** you may wish to call them.

Their motto is, "If you do **THIS** for me I'll do **THAT** for you." Believe me, it runs to the enth degree. Such as, jobs for their ***sons, daughters, family members, gifts etc.*** Just to get a decision of ***favorable furtherance*** for their causes. Yes, it is ***a most despicably dishonest backhanded system, a two way street,*** not out in the open, but in some ***Judges chambers, private rooms, dinner parties, like a Judge*** stated in the **JOSEPH BORKIN'S** book, **"THE CORRUPT JUDGE." (Clarkson N. Potter.)**

A little background on **Joseph Borkin** .. He served as chief economic adviser and attorney in the **ANTI-TRUST** division of the Department of Justice. His book says … "Payoffs took place **IN BACK ALLEYS AND JUDICIAL CHAMBERS.** At a stroke, the corrupt

Judge substitutes the rule of **FORCE** and **FRAUD** for the, **'Principles of Justice.'**

Page 16 in his book says - -" For a Judge to deviate from the most rigid honesty and impartiality is to betray the integrity of all law."

Page 17 in his book says - - "But a Judge must keep himself absolutely above suspicion,"

"If the Judge becomes beholden to one side, it is plain that the opposing side is no longer equal in the eyes of the deciding Judge."

The American Bar Association recognized the Canons of Professional Ethics that Judicial conduct is a matter of importance far beyond the courtroom.

A Judge, in this book, **was paid *a quarter of a million dollars*** to get a ***good decision*** for a friend. The **law firm** involved was the **Cravath, Swaine and Moore,** in the **Williamsport Wire Rope Co.** The Judge in that case was **ALBERT W.JOHNSON,** of the **United States District Court** for the **Middle District of Pennsylvania.**

"The memory of the score of years that **JOHNSON** sat on the bench, will **ALWAYS** be a **NIGHTMARE** for ***the law enforcement agencies, the bar, the bench of that district*** in **Pennsylvania.** The Judge's car **(Page 175)** was parked down the block from **CRAVATH'S OFFICE** in New York, where he was paid **$250,000.00** for a decision someone desired."

Well years ago, in another action I had in the Courts, my adversaries had engaged **THIS LAW FIRM** to handle their case. With **ME**, as a **Pro Se.** you can just imagine what a time I had trying to get justice with this possible **BUNCH OF CROOKS**!" They were ***notorious*** and obviously knew just how to take care of those, **'PENETRATABLE JUDGES.**

MR. BORKIN'S book, "THE CORRUPT JUDGE," is a terrific expose of many corrupt Judges. It proves the ***feelings*** and ***experiences*** I have had to live with in this court system and what goes on in our **Federal and State Courts.**

This book by **JOSEPH BORKIN,** is ***fantastic.*** It is a ***revelation*** of these **lawyers and Judges.** You know first hand this **sickening nightmare of corruption** on this **'HIGH LEVEL'** is positively ***revolting.*** The **JUDGES** truly **MASSACRE** Justice.

So, where does one go to find a solution to a problem? Certainly **NOT** a **COURTHOUSE!** ***The whole system, from top to bottom, is possibly contaminated*** with their ***deal making*** and ***contrivances.***

Woe befalls the person who engages ***a lawyer.*** **THAT** is the beginning. **THAT** is the ***first step*** to set these admittedly **'CRAFTY BLOOD SUCKERS'** into action. And then the other **maneuvering contrivers** of the **truth,** corral their **BROTHERS IN CRIME**, who they owe some past allegiances to, for **'FAVORS'** well done for them.

How sad that the public is not wise to their underhanded self serving deceitful decisions. Many are aware, but what can they do, with ***these crooks at the helm steering their ships into muddy waters?***

Possibly these Judges and lawyers have warped minds which are twisted with deals. Honesty does not for one moment enter into their dubious decision making. They ***circumvent*** the facts. They have the ***proclivity*** of

turning words in their ***direction*** to make ***their*** point. **YOU,** do not count…..

The last sitting Surrogate Judge who allegedly signed his ***'honorable'*** name to a paper that his compatriot wrote and composed, could not have had the knowledge of the dealings and the glorification of these perpetrators who lied **under oath.** The **Ex-Judge,** now the **lawyer** for **my adversary,** who by the way was a ***surrogate Judge*** for some ***fifteen years*** on that same bench. He is the one who apparently wrote this decision and the **two year Judge** on the bench, evidently signed it!

It is a ***conspiracy, a racket,*** a system wholly for the benefit of the ***Judges*** and the ***lawyers*** to scheme out their ***prearranged misguided*** and ***disease laden,*** court system.

It is the distortion of the true seeking ***of justice*** for anyone entering ***this travesty, this desecration, this notorious pervasion,*** by these man made **'GODS'** in their **'BLACK ROBED REGALIA.'** Yes, **THEY** are **wicked, THEY** are **EVIL, THEY** are **UNJUST, THEY** are the **'Men of Darkness,'** under those **black irreligious cloaks.**

Now, with the power they are endowed with, because of the donning of those ***bedeviled Black Robes,*** they truly become **MEPHISTOPHELIAN** ***demons.*** They are **Possessed** with their powers. After all, do you not address these villains as, **'Your Honor?' DARN IT**, it disgusts me to call them, ***'Your Honor.'*** They are the most **HONOR-LESS'** ***creatures*** who ***walk this planet!***

THEY are the **epitome of failure** to the human race. **THEY** are the ***miscarriage of justice.*** **THEY** are the ***downfall*** *and* ***ruination of honesty.*** *Whatever happened to that phrase,* **"DO UNTO OTHERS AS YOU WOULD HAVE THEM DO UNTO YOU?"**

Their **KARMA** is bankrupt of **honesty** and **kindness,** and when, on their declining day of reckoning, and ***all the EVIL they have done to good people*** will be ***tallied***, the wishes of **all those** that they ***hurt*** with their ***dishonest courtroom procedures,*** their **ominous** deeds on earth will certainly be rewarded with **the torture** we all have suffered at their '**Blood Filled Hands.'**

Let us not for one moment, forget their families and loved ones who obviously ***partook*** of the ***EVIL disobedience,*** to their oath in office. They too will suffer. Did they not drink of the ***nectar*** and ***wines*** that these culprits brought back to their ***lairs,*** to share with their loved ones? Their **furs,** their ***vacations,*** their ***wining*** and ***dining***...all this brought about by their ***avaricious greed*** and their ***sabotaging the Truths.***

These **benched bandits** in their ***Black Evil robes,*** are **commensurate** *to* **stealing**, when they hand down a ***biased decision*** that was given ***Birth*** to, in their private chambers with and for his cohorts, and of course the possible affixing of his name to a document that was written by his friend **(an Ex-Judge),** who sat on the bench for many years before this new (**two- year present Judge.**) I do not believe he obviously read this ***many page document*** before he put his name on, **THE PUTNAM HEARING.**

A Judge is the same as a ***rapist***, a ***thief.*** He is stealing Your Justice in a case you unfortunately have **before him. A bandit and such-In days of old, would have been** ***tarred*** **and** ***feathered,*** **placed in a stockade**

in the middle of town for all to see. No questions asked, and then **S H O T**!!! Well now, **IS HE NOT A THEIF, A PICK POCKET ON A LARGER SCALE?**

Not only is this **'BLACK ROBED RIP OFF ARTIST'** denying you what is rightfully yours, but at the same time he is recompensed by his cronies. Yes, he is **REWARDED** from all sides for **F…K…, (SCREWING YOU!) Ah, yes,** they are the biggest ***swindlers, embezzlers, plunderers, massacres*** of the ***truth,*** to line their pockets and that of their cohorts.

These ***dispensers*** of so called, ***tailor made justice,*** from their wooden benches and wooden gavels, are merchants. They are apparently brokers in, **"Pay For Your Decision…"** They massacre their decrees for their friends. They were shyster lawyers and ambulance chasers before they worked themselves up in the "**POLITICAL PARTIES**."

Running errands for the Bosses, putting posters around the stores, to curry favor so they could one day too, **GET A PIECE OF THE ACTION.** ***Yes, it is a "hand kissing", back stabbing business*** and, We are the poor souls that they do it to….

I truly put it on the agenda, to write and educate you, doing my best to curtail your disappointment in our **'JUDICIAL SYSTEM.'** I still feel ridiculous addressing them as, **'YOUR HONOR.'**

Now, I do not say they are ***ALL*** **the same, that they are all deal makers,** but I have had the **DISPLEASURE** and experience with both **lawyers** and **Judges … FOUR TIMES.** I have **SEEN** ***so much,*** and I have **LEARNED so much!**

But take heed. The only thing that **these 'PURVEYORS OF INJUSTICE,'** is the **EVIL** they have done to us, with their paid-for dishonest decisions. They will take nothing but their ***rotten lying bodies*** into the nether world. They are destined to ***writhe*** in **Hell,** through ***Eternity.***

Their spirits will probably never find ***rest,*** for the ***torture*** they inflicted on us and especially upon **ME.** They will suffer for every tear **WE** shed because of their possibly paid-for ***dishonest decisions.*** Their ***mean bones*** will never rest in ***peace.*** They will grovel on the coals of **HELL** for what they put us through.

Whenever I went to court (***that house of ill repute),*** all I wanted was what was rightfully mine. As a plaintiff, **THEY** were bought off to throw my cases or drag them out. Well I did have some ***gilt- edged law firms*** for my ***opposition,*** and you know very well how those decisions were made.

So-they had their chances to be **honest**....But, **those favors** and **those payoffs** were **too good** and too ***lucrative*** for them **NOT** to throw my case. Well the **DEVIL,** will now reward them, **"JUSTLY"**

HOW DISGUSTING IT ALWAYS WAS FOR ME TO SAY....

"YOUR HONOR!!!'

I CANNOT BELIEVE THAT THESE SUPPOSEDLY INTELLIGENT, COLLEGE

EDUCATED GRADUATES, CAN BE SO BRUTAL AS TO WATCH THAT PERSON STANDING BEFORE THEM, SUFFER BECAUSE OF THEIR POSSIBLE BIASED, PAID FOR DECISIONS, WHO DO NOT STRESS HONESTY, AND TO SEEK A VIABLE SOLUTION TO A PROBLEM, INSTEAD OF TARNISHING THE TRUTH AND THE JUST.

I QUIERY,

JUST HOW BRAVE

<u>ARE</u> THESE JUDGES

WITHOUT THEIR DIRTY

.....BLACK....

.SHROUDS,....

POSSIBLY COVERING,

THEIR

SINS???..

CHAPTER-TWELVE

"LOOKING BACK"

Looking ***back*** to the ***beginning*** of this case, I shall remember the ***first impressions*** I felt of the ***sitting Judge.*** He, ***at the start,*** seemed to be ***kind,*** at least I wanted to think so, but he quickly changed my mind when he repeatedly said those oft said ***sick words*** – **"GET A LAWYER,"** (after all this while, I now ***understand,*** and know the **reason** why they hate to deal with a **Pro-Se**.)

You see, the ***lawyers*** on ***both sides*** can convene in the ***Judges chambers*** or over a ***cocktail,*** and hammer out their deals, whereas with a **Pro-Se** (that is me, a person, ***not*** a lawyer, but representing my own case), it would be ***impossible*** for them to carry out their ***usual shtick! (clandestine meetings!)***

This is the routine among these ***'legal-ites'*** I am so sure ***he was well aware, and knew only too well,*** what his **compatriots** were obviously doing to me. ***Harassment, lies, duplicity and stealing my rights.*** After all, who am I to come into their **'Pristine Courtroom'** and ***expect to get, and receive, my honest and well deserved justice*** in this ***bon fide case.***

Well, there were also those ***loving souls*** that were standing beside me. Yes, I was so very much aware of ***my dear sweet mother's presence,*** and, of course, the ***Lord*** who also guides me, to bear ***witness*** to what they were doing to me. I sensed it so very ***positively.*** It is a most ***overpowering sensation,*** and I suddenly felt ***calm*** with this feeling.

For the ***torture*** and ***stealing*** and ***lies*** that kept swirling around, I just knew ***these charlatans*** who were putting on this ***cruel act,*** were building **<u>their very own</u>** **KARMIC DEBT,** to astronomical proportions.

When I think, that all I ever do is care for and be kind to everyone who comes in contact with me, and here in **<u>this court case,</u>** it was **<u>returned</u>** to **<u>me</u>** with **<u>jealousy</u>** and **<u>hate!</u>** A lesson I am learning, is not to give so much caring and not to be so concerned about others, who in return reciprocate my sincerity by repaying me with **<u>lies,</u>** **<u>stealing</u>** and **<u>deliberately hurting me.</u>**

The lawyers and Judges have done this kind of business in this court before, so actually it is **BUSINESS AS USUAL.** It must be a terrible thing to happen to them for a **<u>Pro Se,</u>** **<u>like me,</u>** to possibly mess up their **<u>dirty dishonest agenda</u>** and making their plans a **<u>shambles for them.</u>**

They do not know how to ***deal*** with me. I am well aware of their **wheeling** and ***dealing*** that takes place out of their ***clients*** presence. These so called **<u>people</u>** of **<u>the court</u>** have **<u>lies</u>** and ***<u>maneuverings</u>*** and ***<u>cover-ups</u>*** on their side, whereas, I have ***<u>honesty,</u>*** ***<u>integrity,</u>*** a ***<u>fine up bringing</u>*** <u>with</u> ***<u>honest values,</u>*** and the dear **<u>Lord</u>** to **<u>guide me.</u>**

So, if I do not get the ***justice*** I ***deserve*** in this case, something ***good*** will come to me to ***repay me*** for their ***deceit and thievery.*** Oh, they will pay **heavily and big time,** because, ***everything evens out,*** nothing ever goes by ***unrequited*** with fate.

Yes, unfortunately in the ***four cases*** I sought to find ***justice*** in this ***manufactured court system,*** I learned ***a lot.*** My own ***well paid lawyers*** at ***that time,*** were getting ***paid off*** from my ***adversaries*** to **THROW MY CASES.** I will tell you more in another book what I have been through with these so called '**OFFICERS OF THE COURT!**" Yes, my ***own lawyers*** were deal making with the other side and **getting fees** from me as well. So, this ***taught*** me to do it ***myself,*** at least I know what is going on.

~AND THAT IS THE CATASTROPHE FOR THE 'HONORABLE' COURT SYSTEM-

~THEY CAN'T STAND TO DEAL WITH~

..... PRO SES .....

LIKE ME!

~I PROVED TO THEM THAT I WAS NOT ONE TO BE TAMPERED WITH, OR TO BE PLOYED AND TOYED WITH, BECAUSE EVEN THOUGH I DID NOT HAVE A LAW DEGREE, I KNEW IN MY HEART THAT I MUST FIGHT MY CASE WITH EVERY OUNCE OF INTELLIGENCE AND KNOWLEDGE THAT GOD GAVE ME. I COULD ALREADY SEE THE HANDWRITING ON THE WALL, AND IT SURE WAS A BLUR!

I WAS NOT ABOUT TO PLAY THEIR GAME OR EVEN BE PART OF IT. I SIMPLY REFUSE TO DO BUSINESS

~ WITH .... THE DEVIL! ~

CHAPTER -THIRTEEN

"MY JOURNEY AS A PLAINTIFF IN FEDERAL AND STATE COURTS"

~AND THOSE WHO HAVE INTENTIONALLY FALSIFIED EVIDENCE IN THESE CASES HAVE EVOKED, ETERNAL DAMNATION.....

My experience in **Federal Courts** and most recently the New York State Surrogate Court is simply this: The ***judges and lawyers*** are a, ***"self serving community,"*** which seems to operate under a Black cloak of **spurious respectability** and **immunity** from **public retribution.**

The lawyers are for the most part primarily ***business men without scruples:*** not above outright **Bribery** or **Exchange of favors,** whichever promotes the short term or long term success of the business. And, if these lawyers are of service to the ***prevailing political machine,*** they secure nominations for ***New York Judicial office,*** which assures election. The next step is an appointment to ***permanent Federal Judgeship*.**

It is attained by developing similar service to the **Federal Bureaucracy,** including the **President of the United States.**

The **machinery** for **judicial discipline** at both levels is a ***failure,*** because it is **self-policing** and is ***isolated from direct public referendum.*** The **weak link** in adjudication of a charge of ***Federal misconduct*** is the **CHIEF JUDGE** of the ***judicial circuit,*** who has the last word and who is possibly <u>**NOT**</u> above **unlawful inducement.**

President Harry Truman proudly declared, "**THE BUCK STOPS HERE,"** in this present day, it is more than a buck, and it **DOESN'T STOP ANYWHERE**. **The State Judicial Disciplinary Agency,** is a voluntary association of lawyers, without power to ***censure*** or ***remove*** an ***offending lawyer or Judge.***

The consequence of ***media concealment*** and ***public referendum*** exclusion, is a ***progressive degradation of judicial competence, integrity, and loss of public confidence,*** in the possibly ***plundered court system. This*** inevitably leads to antagonism between the **AMERICAN PUBLIC AND IT'S OWN GOVERNMENT**!

If in the past, you have been a victim of ***biased courts,*** please do not think ***you are alone.*** It has been ***done to others*** and, to ***ME.*** We have been **SILENT LONG ENOUGH**! The court officers are public servants, and the controlling statutes must be written to serve that public interest ***without the intervention of mercenaries,*** with ***over flowing human weakness.***

And so I say, is it better to tell the ***truth*** in a ***small dusty courtroom,*** filled with ***contrivances*** and **intrigue,** with your enemies ready to ***pounce on*** you because you are telling the ***truth*** as it really is, or, is it better to tell it to ***the world,*** to those who ***have suffered*** many times over in a place such as this, where ***dishonesty, mystically Rules the day?***

I know first hand in a courtroom like this last one that may have **MASSACRED**, **LIED** and did not permit the **TRUTH** to see the light of day in that **SMELLY,**

DINGY PLACE. It was *reeling* and ***wheeling*** with ***disgust,*** and ***disgrace.*** **AWFUL! SIMPLY AWFUL!**

They almost seem to ***defy*** you, they don't want to hear the ***truth***, they ***shut*** you up. I see now that is not the place for the truth to be heard, because you are inevitably messing up their ***neatly planned agenda.***

I must say it is a ***sad joke.*** Anyone who goes to court to find ***justice*** is ***fooling themselves.*** It is a pity – a pity how it is camouflaged. The truth dies and is buried in that place. That place that has more Evil goings on with the blessing of our Beautiful ***American Flag*** that stands behind the Judge and possibly watches ***all the corrupt, deceitful*** lies and injustices that take place. So many have given their precious lives for it, in order that these so called ***legal culprits*** can freely hold court and desecrate the men who fought honorably for ***Justice and Freedom.***

And that is precisely what happens there in those **ROOMS** where our dear **American Flags** are used as a **COVER UP**….. .. "See we are ***hones***t, we are working for **American justice." HA! WHAT A JOKE!**

The minute you put your foot inside a courthouse, you very possibly are a ***gambler.*** It matters ***not*** if you have an **HONEST AIR-TIGHT CASE**, and you are a righteous person seeking your justice. **Well, forget it!! Don't delude yourself** – you do not know the shenanigans that have transpired before you arrived there; ***Who did what, Who knew who***, and of course ***what favors were promised***. It is like knowing which horse will win the race before the race is won, and I can vouch for that. I know, I've been **THERE BEFORE**. **THEY HAVE DONE IT TO ME.**

THIS PRACTICE, THIS SCAM is very likely going on in the other courtrooms in America. **YES**, a place that is supposed to ***lend credence, honesty*** and ***respectability.*** **THE DEVIL PROBABLY SITS THERE BESIDE THE JUDGE**, ***taking notes, breathing it all in***, watching the ***tempting lure of favors*** and other ***morsels of enticement,*** **TO THROW A CASE.** When you are in the courtroom, it is **A PHONY FRONT COVER UP.** The decisions are flagrantly already in the **"BAG,"** with **WHATEVER ELSE IS IN IT**. The **decisions** were well reached in chambers **(the place where you and I cannot go),** ***dinner parties, social events and favors.***

It has happened several times to me. I had good honest **BONAFIDE** cases – and I never got the **JUSTICE** I deserved and had sought. One case was dismissed without my day in court, after I waited years to have my case heard. **THE LAWYER FOR THE OTHER SIDE WAS RIGHT ACROSS THE STREET FROM THE COURTHOUSE**. **BOY THAT WAS SOME CASE, AND THE JUDGE SQUASHED IT. SO JUSTICE AGAIN WAS NOT SERVED, NOR DID IT SEE THE LIGHT OF DAY!** ....

When I will be interviewed, I will go into some of these travesties that took place in those dishonorable surroundings.

So I say, "**WHY ME LORD? WHY AM I THE CHOSEN ONE** to write about this farce, to tell about the corruption in this sick system?" They constantly say to me – **"GET A LAWYER- GET A LAWYER!"**

Well, I have had some in the past. Deals were made with my, '**so called lawyers.'** **YES, THEY**

VICIOUSLY SOLD ME OUT. At least as a **Pro Se,** I can see just what is going on! **DISHONESTY!......** They cannot handle me or make deals with the lawyers that I would engage, as they did in the past. There is a saying, **"THERE IS NO HONOR AMONG THIEVES"**.....

Boy this is some business where the deal making runs rampant. **FACTS DO NOT COUNT. IT IS STRICTLY A BARTARING SYSTEM!** Such as, "**IF YOU GIVE MY SON, OR RELATIVE OR WHOEVER** , a job, in one of your law firms, I will see that the decision you seek, is **A FAVORABLE ONE** for you." It will be in the **'BAG,'** so as to say. And I can say it **WAS APPARENTLY** in the '**BAG'** in the Federal Court on Foley Square, and elsewhere!

In this the first case I had a while back when the lawyers who I had engaged to handle ***an anti-trust case*** for me, ***(because I did not have this experience then, and trusted those culprits),*** who took my money, and favors from the other side, to throw this action, which was a **VERY BIG ONE**.

Sadly, it is a ***miserable way*** to get justice. Justice, I find is a corrupt system-it is in total control. I do not have ***one enemy*** in all the world, now I have a ***new gang,*** and a **GANG** it is. The ***Public Administrator,*** who is obviously supposed to be ***totally impartial,*** is hanging out with the ***other side.*** They have done some conspicuously criminal dealings in this case. There is ***much dishonesty*** running wild with the possible ***'Blessings,'*** of the **Court System.**

I never thought I could put all of this intrigue down on paper, but look, I am writing about it, **YES.** Now, my experience in this particular contrived case, obviously **(contrived by my adversaries)** is **shocking.** The dishonesty is rampant, and running wild in this **Surrogate case.** The world must know what I've been through and what goes on in these buildings where **JUSTICE IS possibly SLAUGHTERED!**

Now, if I had been treated honestly and would have gotten the proper justice that is supposed to be dealt with in this courthouse, instead of this **GRUESOME NIGHTMARE** that I have experienced here, **PERHAPS BY EACH OF THE WITNESSES,'** lying under oath. While I had proof of the untruths **COMING FORTH** from their mouths, after taking the oath over the ***Bible*** and in front of the ***American Flag,*** I would not be writing now.

But, the Judge did **NOT** permit me to contradict them and would **NOT** let me introduce my proofs. I had engaged a **Bona fide Handwriting Expert** – I had signed proof by notaries, **YET THE JUDGE WOULD NOT LET ME INTRODUCE THEM.** I saw the deal I had to contend with. The Ex-Judge who sat on this same bench for many years, now coming back as a lawyer, in the same court for the defendant ***(while his picture, when he was a judge in the same courtroom, still hangs high on this wall.*** **HOW ABOUT THAT?)**

Apparently the Judge on the bench, hearing this case, and this Ex-Judge, now turned lawyer, can converse on the phone or have lunch, or play a round of golf, or who knows what else. Do you think the Judge on the bench would talk to me or converse on the phone? Would he have lunch with me? **NO!, NO!, NO!**

So you see, the public does not know what discernibly goes on in their chambers, and we, are at their mercy. They do what they please, and the decisions are **very likely, TAILOR MADE**. Eyes and ears cannot be a part of this sick **JUSTICE with EX-JUDGES** coming back into the court system as lawyers, **in the very same courtroom where they presided before. WOW! ANYTHING TO GREASE THE WAY**.

You often hear, ***"My son, the Lawyer, My husband the Judge."*** What pride can the families of these villains, who play **GOD** in those **'BLACK ROBES' (to possibly hide their dishonesty.)** How many people have been hurt with no recourse by these revered counselors dispensing **THEIR** kind of justice, who are addressed as, **'YOUR HONOR?'**

But have no fear, these people who **'TOY'** with ***yours and other peoples lives, and cause you a lot of unnecessary pain and heartache,*** they are building a great story in the ***Lord's good book.***

Some of those who did not do right by me in my other cases, they had ***their day of reckoning.*** All those who did not play fair in the past, they know best how their dishonesty to me has paid off for them.

So, on **THEIR DAY** ***of departure, from this world of chaos, (which they did their best to make)*** and they knock on the **DEVIL'S DOOR** down below, they will be greeted like this:

"I HAVE AWAITED YOUR ARRIVAL. I'VE KEPT A BOOK FULL OF NOTES OF ALL YOUR WHEELINGS AND DEALINGS, YOUR DEEDS, THE HAVOC YOU RAISED IN OTHER PEOPLES'

LIVES, THE HURTS YOU CAUSED OTHER HUMANS- HAVE EARNED YOU YOUR SPECIAL PLACE OF DIS-HONOR HERE. BESIDES, I'VE GOT A COUPLE OF SURPRISES FOR YOU.

MANY OF YOUR LEGAL CRONIES ARE WAITING FOR YOU TOO. SO, MAKE YOURSELF AT HOME, HANG YOUR BLACK ROBE NEXT TO THEIRS IN THE CLOAK ROOM, AND LEARN MY RULES, WHICH ARE QUITE SIMPLE. I AM THE JUDGE DOWN HERE.....YOUR INHUMANE DEMERITS ARE OVERFLOWING. THERE ARE NO APPEALS, THERE ARE NO PAY-OFFS. YOUR NOISY GAVEL STOPS HERE. BANG IT ON YOUR HEAD IF YOU WANT, ONLY I WILL SEE IT. I DON'T CARE HOW LONG YOU WANT TO BANG IT. I AM THE ONLY ONE YOU CANNOT IMPRESS, AND THOSE WHO YOU HAVE DESECRATED IN THE PAST WILL BE THE ONLY ONES WHO WILL HEAR IT. BANG AWAY AS LONG AS YOU LIKE. THE LONGER , THE BETTER. IF YOU NEED ANY HELP, I WILL ONLY BE TOO HAPPY TO DO IT FOR YOU. HA! HA! HA! YOU BLACK ROBED BANDIT.

You Judges sure had it made up there. You all got away with running rough shod over those who came to you looking for justice in your court. Your unsuspecting public, stood before you believing you were honest and would give them an un-biased decision from you tainted **DIS-HONORABLE BENCH! Sadly, your courtroom reeked of lies, deceit, unjust deals, and corruption.** ***The injustice to those innocent and decent people were***

so great, a most nauseating stench emitted from there because of your wrong doing. It was so pungent an odor that **I could smell it ALL THE WAY DOWN HERE!**

Well, this is **MY** courtroom . Here **I AM** the Judge, and you will now get a taste of your own treatment. What you did to those hapless people who came to you for an **HONEST DECISION, who TRUSTED** you, who **DEPENDED** on you for **JUSTICE,** only to find out about your **EVIL, WICKED, DEAL MAKING**. Well, you will **NOW PAY. THIS IS YOUR WRETCHED AND AWFUL SENTENCE THAT YOU HAVE EARNED WITH YOUR COURTROOM CONDUCT. THERE IS NO ESCAPE FOR YOUR POOR DOOMED SOUL.**

Tell me, **MY MOST DISHONORABLE ONE**, how does it feel not to be heard? **TO PLEAD YOUR CASE BEFORE ME AND I WILL NOT LISTEN TO YOU?** This is how you **CONDUCTED THOSE CASES** in your courtroom.... Make yourself at home and get ready for your **EARNED PAYOFF.** I now would like you to enjoy some of the treatment you inflicted on all those ***poor helpless people***, who trusted you and their lawyer to give an **HONEST DECISION** in their cases. You sure did a great job breaking people's hearts when **YOU RULED ON THE BENCH**. By the way, I do hope you are uncomfortable on these **HOT COALS** that you are sitting on. If you need some **MORE HEAT**, just ask, it would be no problem for me to **MAKE IT AS HOT FOR YOU** as you made it for those people who stood before you. You belong to **ME** now, you are under **MY** control, so any request you may have, please feel free to <u>**BELCH OUT**</u> your desires. I would be only too happy to oblige. **I AM SORRY, IT IS NOT LIKE THAT SOFT, CUSHY, BENCH** you used to sit on when you carried out your backroom deals in your courthouse.

Another thing, <u>**YOU**</u> do not call the shots down here! <u>**I WON'T BE BRIBED.**</u> Down here, you are on your own and no one will plead your case for you. By the way, some of your old crony pals gave me an earful about your scheming deal making and they were not very nice. **WHY DID YOU SELL YOUR SOUL TO ME?** Too bad you cannot take this heat even though it is not as hot yet, as you made it for some of those who expected justice before your **BLACK ROBES.** You have brought great **'DISHONOR TO THE TITLE.'**

With your conduct in the American Court System, you automatically traded your bench for this **HOT SEAT.** Did you not think of your day of reckoning or were all those deals from the lawyers coming **FAST** and **FURIOUS**?

What a shame your family did not know the deals you pulled off with those friends of yours in the **BACKROOMS OR DINNER PARTIES, FOR THOSE TAILORED MADE DECISIONS AND FAVORS.** You will all meet and blame each other for you reservations down here in **HADES.** Now, if you can't take all this heat , there is no other place for you to go, so please, stop the **CRAP** and get **USED** to the misery.

You all worked so tediously and dishonestly in order to ensure your entry and occupy your first class seats in this devilish pit. Again, I say to you all,

WELCOME! WELCOME, to a place, where you will be showered with all the sparks and **EMBERS** you have so **JUSTLY EARNED**. **THIS,** is what you worked so hard for, while you sat on that bench, for all those years. Did you think you could get away with the **SINS you have COMMITTED? THIS, IS YOUR PURGATORY,…. THIS, IS YOUR SENTENCE.**

I have been waiting and I have reserved this very nice **HOT SEAT,** just for you right next to our **ATOMIC FURNACE. YOU** have made it so **HOT** for so many that stood before you in your courtroom, I only think you deserve the best for ***your possibly devious treatment to them.*** Your decisions broke their hearts, and one more thing, **MY MOST DISHONORABLE ONE,** you won't be needing your **BLACK ROBES** down here. So remember, **HERE I AM THE JUDGE.** You have nothing more to say. You will not be addressed anymore as, **'YOUR HONOR!'** Your **'HONOR,'** is **NOW** a **'GONER.' THESE ARE MY RULES, TAKE IT AS IT COMES, because you do not have the same PRIVILEGES as you had on TOP SIDE.**

Do you remember what you did to that **LITTLE BLOND LADY,** who was **Pro Se,** in that Surrogate action? It was a most heinous sin the way she was treated by all, the **Ex-Judge,** now **Lawyer, the Public Administrator, the self-made Executor,** and all **those that lied.** The treatment everyone gave her to cover up all their lies, was **MOST OUTRAGEOUS** and downright **UNFAIR.** You refused to listen to even **ONE WORD SHE SAID**. She had the **THREE WILLS** which were **ANALYZED** by a **REPUTABLE**

HANDWRITING EXPERT. He said only the **FIRST WILL** was **LEGITIMATE** and that the other **TWO WILLS,** which were written **TEN DAYS APART,** were phonies, so you will **ALL PAY** for the **SINS** you **COMMITTED** against her.

And now, I will read **YOUR RIGHTS** to you, as a matter of fact, **YOU HAVE NO RIGHTS** anymore. I've gotten a **FULL REPORT** on your conduct, and you do not have any **APPEALS** available to you. **THERE ARE NO PAY-OFFS HERE.** All your **DISHONEST DECISIONS** and **THEY ARE MANY,** your **PLEADINGS** and **TEARS** for any reprieve or sympathy have been wiped out. The **TEARS** that fell from the many broken hearts of those who received **YOUR BIASED** and **UNJUST** treatment, washed away any chances, **FOR MERCY!** So tell me, my most **DISHONORABLE ONE, WAS IT WORTH IT?** How does it feel being on the **RECEIVING END? OH,** how **YOUR VICTIMS CRIED** because of those possible **PAID OFF DECISIONS,** ***(you and your lawyer friends decided on.)*** **YES,** come to think of it, some of those lawyers are **COOLING THEIR HEELS** in another part of this **HELLISH HOTEL HOLE.**

Sorry, there is **NO RUNNING WATER** down here, **NO MAID SERVICE, NO CLEAN TOWELS** (only the ones filled with the **BLOOD STAINED TEARS** of your victims.) Also your **DIRTY BLACK SMELLY ROBES,** the ones your WORE when you probably made your **BIASED** decisions. We do not have a **PICK-UP** and **DELIVERY CLEANING SERVICE** either. Besides **YOU NEVER CAME CLEAN** with the **FACTS ANYWAY.** It was always some **CHEAP,**

DIRTY DEALINGS. You should be used to this. This is how **YOU CONDUCTED** business in your court. **YOU EARNED ALL OF THESE MISERIES**.....and now it is all **COMING** back to **YOU.**

It is **AMAZING** that the **MAJORITY OF INHABITANTS** down here are conspicuously **LAWYERS** AND **JUDGES.** They seem to **CORNER THE MARKET** of **DISHONESTY!** I think it is a **CONTAGIOUS DISEASE** – **THIS GREED**. To think those **CLOAKED ONES** feel that they can possibly play **GOD** on their bench, but down here, **I WILL SHOW THEM WHO IS THE BOSS.**

They will **SWEAT IT OUT** (literally) throughout **ETERNITY. There is no road GOING UP or GOING OUT.** Every road is a **DEAD END CUL-DE-SAC,** and they have burnt all their **BRIDGES.** They must now **ROT** with the **EVIL** they **FOMENTED** and with **EVERY DIRTY DEAL THEY PULLED ON THE UNSUSPECTING PUBLIC.** For their **ACTS** in the past, they **MUST- AND SHALL PAY.** They have created their own **'HELL ON EARTH,'** so they should be used to this down here. **AND,** I will show them **NO MERCY**. Did **YOU** ever show **MERCY** to **ANYONE** in your courtroom? The answer is a **BIG EMPHATIC NO.**

I've got to get another **FURNACE** going. I understand the **LAW COLLEGES JUST GRADUATED SOME NEW ONES, THOUSANDS MORE,** and before you know it, they will be **JUDGES AND NOW YOU KNOW** where most of them will **WIND UP....DOWN HERE!!!**

And if you great legal minds think this can't happen, **THINK AGAIN.** I am living proof of the system, whether I had expensive lawyers or fought my case as a **Pro Se,** especially the **DISHONESTY** and **TRICKERY,** the **WILL CHANGING,** the **STEALING** and the **FORGERY THAT WENT ON IN THIS LAST CASE.**

All of you who are involved, are **NEXT IN LINE** for the **ROYAL** treatment from the **DEVIL,** for what you have done to me- a **PROPER, HONEST LADY** doing good deeds to all that come into my **PATH,** helping people – unfortunate people setting them **STRAIGHT** on the **TRUE MEANING OF LIFE**- encouraging- **NO SMOKING, NO DRINKING** – teaching them about all the helpful diets – being honest and kind to people and **GOD'S** little creatures and YET, you all **CHEATED ME AND ILL-TREATED ME, MOCKED ME** in every which way, manner, shape or form. MY MISSION is to do good in this life, which is a test. **Everything evens out, THE GOOD YOU DO AND THE BAD YOU DO. Nothing goes UNPUNISHED OR UNANSWERED.**

YOU HAVE NO ONE TO BLAME BUT YOURSELVES……..(IT POSSIBLY COULD BE THAT AIR ON STATEN ISLAND.)……

PERHAPS IT MUST BE THE REASON I COULD NOT GET ANY LAWYER TO TAKE MY CASE…… BECAUSE WHEN I SPOKE TO THOSE LAWYERS FROM STATEN ISLAND, THEY SAID:

WE DO OUR BUSINESS IN THAT COURT AND WE DO NOT WANT TO

..........BUCK

..........THOSE

..........GUYS!.........

THE JUDGE KEPT TELLING ME TO GET A LAWYER, INFACT HE GAVE ME SEVERAL WEEKS TO FIND ONE. HE FINALLY ASKED ME IF I DID FIND ONE. I TOLD HIM, "THE LAWYERS ON LONG ISLAND SAID IT WAS TOO FAR TO GO, AND THE ONES IN NEW YORK CITY SAID, WE DON'T CARE TO GO THERE BECAUSE IT IS:

A CLOSED.......

SHOP".......

CHAPTER-FOURTEEN

"MARCH 12, 2000"
~ "THAT OTHER DAY OF INFAMY" ~

When this case is finally over, **(and it cannot be soon enough for me,) then and only then**, **heralds** the beginning for what has ***transpired*** for this length of time, in this **APPARENTLY SLANTED COURT,** and it **WAS** and **IS** by **NO MEANS, AN ACCIDENT.**

YOU, yes **EACH** and **EVERYONE** of you, have you **NOT** ***wondered, pondered, questioned, asked yourself,*** what **IS** and what **WAS** this all about?

From the ***Judge,*** his **henchmen,** his ***stooges,*** his ***attendants*** and his ***puppets; all the people in that courthouse,*** and those ***uniformed searchers*** you are possibly confronted with, when you enter that courthouse. They greet you with their dour expressions, they search your pockets, your attaché case, and your personal belongings. They open it all to possibly reveal a tape recorder or a weapon. Such is the distrust and honesty that takes place within the walls of this most ***'Pristine Courthouse!'*** ***(*****They would possibly do better if they did their POLICING in the JUDGES CHAMBERS.)**

Oh, if only those walls in his chambers could ***talk*** and also in the open court **(which is really a closed court,) NOTHING,** but **NOTHING** must be let out of the ***building*** for the public to see.

Now all of you, stop to think, why have we all been brought together in this case? The answer came to me while I was feeding all the birds at my home. I have no doubt from the Judge down, **WHY WE HAVE BEEN THROWN TOGETHER IN THIS MASSACRED, AND WELL MASSAGED CASE OF MY FRIEND, AND HIS WILLS. Also ALFONSO D'ARTEGA, the GREAT COMPOSER** who has led the ***prominent musicians*** such as the **New York Philharmonic, Rome, Milan, London, Miami, Buffalo and the NBC Symphony Orchestra** and has written many musical compositions amongst which is the very famous, **"In the Blue of the Evening."**

KARMA has definitely arranged for this cast to be brought together in this melodrama, and if you doubt it, do be honest to yourselves ***(although after watching you in action, I think that quite impossible.)*** All of you will see just what I mean.

Let us start with **Bernard's** passing. That poor soul with his lifetime of ***drinking and smoking,*** did stop those bad habits on weekends, when he came out to my home. His next door neighbor, ***the many hat-ted contriving lawyer, money grubber,*** and his **MANY VARIED WILLS;** his secretary who obviously specializes in **CUSTOM MADE ERRORS** on pertinent documents; his little convenient wife, who dutifully serves the coffee, **(which who knows what was in it,)** and she does not remember a thing except for signing a **WILL** with her name on it. **WHO, WHERE, WHAT OR WHEN,** does not matter, as long as she says it the way her husband, **THE WILL WRITER,** has apparently coached her to say. Of course, we have the lawyer for the two next door ***fighting neighbors.*** This lawyer jumped up to object to every question I asked ***his clients.*** I did not even have the ***second word*** out of my mouth and they were already objecting. When **Bernard** came out on weekends, he told us he could hear the ***name calling*** they did. The walls were ***so thin*** in those huts, the ***dirty cussing words*** they called each other was ***awful.***

Then there were several others involved, who were playing their parts to ***the hilt.*** And now we have the short appearance of the Ex-Judge, who obviously warmed that same bench in that same courtroom for some ***fifteen years.*** He was brought into this case by the lawyer to save ***his neck, (and his—-other parts)*** because I wanted the **TRUTHS** about those **PHONY WILLS.** By the way, his picture hung on the wall in that courtroom for all his ***fifteen years,*** even though mystically, he no longer made his decision ***as a Judge. (They should have probably hung this creep by his ,,,……… along with his picture.)***

So now, he is the lawyer for the ***contrived*** **EXECUTOR/WILL WRITER.** Well **HE** apparently wrote the decision for the **PUTNAM HEARING**…. and the ***sitting Judge*** obviously signed it!!! His untruths in this paper were il-legal. I do not know what possible pressure he still has over the sitting Judge of just two years, but it was nice of him to get the Ex-Judge into this case to earn a couple of **BUCKS** – about **$3,500.00,** which the Executor wants the Beneficiaries to pay. **HOW ABOUT THAT! Oh SHAME OF SHAMES. (But this goes on and it's done behind the public's un-awareness.)**

Well, one day this **Ex-Judge quits this case, (and his picture which hung on the wall, left with him.) HOW, WHY, THE MYSTERY THICKENS….This Ex-Judge** apparently wrote this **BIASED** decision and the present presiding Judge obviously signed it!!! **(SPECIFICALLY LEAVING OUT PROVISION #4 IN THE TWO CONTRIVED WILLS, TEN DAYS APART. THAT PUTNAM** paper was a ***deliberate disgrace.*** He left out the ***main witness*** who was the only one that told the **TRUTH** – that the deceased was a member in **ALCOHOLIC ANONYMOUS** and was an **ALCOHOLIC,** who was very likely taken advantage of by ***this charlatan lawyer.*** The Judge signed his name to this **dishonest document**!

The Judge even commented to **Mr. Lombardi,** – **"YOU WERE THE BEST WITNESS HERE TODAY, THANK YOU FOR COMING."** Yet, **WHY** did he leave out his name and his **TESTIMONY COMPLETELY** from the **PUTNAM REPORT?** They wear those **Black Robes** and they are addressed as **"YOUR HONOR,"** but where does The **HONOR** begin? **(This is one of the lyrics on my CD record.)**

So, the **Ex-Judge** left, ***picture and all, (one down, the rest to go.)*** They are all in on it. The ***Public Administrator***, **(appointed by the Judge),** this ***Surrogate Judge,*** I guess the **DEVIL** entered this picture to keep his touch. So this whole case starts to swing and **THEY DID** and **IT DID!!!**

Now we come to the **MEAT** of this whole **'FIASCO.'** Each of **YOU** and not just **ONE OF YOU,** but **ALL OF YOU** know ***the lies, the plotting*** and exactly what you did to **ME**, in this case of **Bernard's WILL.**

Do you all ***not realize,*** you are being ***tested?*** The ***treatment*** you have ***subjected*** me to, ***your possible lying,***

cheating, deceptions and stealing, for your own ***selfish benefit*** - **YOU WILL BURN!**

When this case first began, I thought we were going to find the **TRUTH.** I smiled to you all when I came into court, but it was not to be. You all **herded** together like ***cattle,*** thinking I was ***so stupid*** not to see your dishonest moves, but **GOD** did see **THAT,** and **MORE.** You were all banded together to fight me because I wanted to find the **'TRUTH,'** but your mission was to **HIDE IT…. It was most obvious**. You all **SLAUGHTERED** the **EVIDENCE** ***bit by bit***. ~ And sadly to say …. With the possible **Blessings of this Court.**

This does not go with my upbringing or background. I will not have any part of it. These falsehoods or these types of people who hide the **TRUTH,** who **STEAL** and who **LIE** and **CHEAT** are a **DISGRACE** to the ***human race.*** It was a sick revelation and a sure giveaway, when you all ***huddled together*** in the hall of the courthouse, plotting how to possibly ***deceive*** me, never to **greet** me. I knew something was very, very wrong.

The way you all treated me was ***abominable,*** and ***most ungodly.*** The lies in the courtroom, after you each took the oath, in front of our **'AMERICAN FLAG,'** was all the proof I needed to make me see what was happening, and that too, with the likely and possible **CONDONATION** of the **COURT.** Yes, I was very much aware of what was going on, and so was the **LORD.**

Well, today I am positive of my role in this courtroom court scene. **I AM A CATALYST.** I am giving you, each one, the chance to explain the ***devilish treatment*** you dished out to me. There is no doubt that your **KARMA** is ***registering for your future,*** because of what you have **DONE** and are **DOING** to **ME.**

YES! your very own future and that of your families are being ***weighed*** and ***tested*** on how you have all ***massacred*** and ***possibly falsified*** the **EVIDENCE**. Now, you **CANNOT** turn the clock back because it is registered against your names in the **KARMIC debt book.** And none of your ***pleadings*** and ***pay-offs,*** can wipe this out. You all ***LIED,*** **LIED** and **LIED** some more, ***until your tongues were hanging out your mouths with sweat dripping off them.*** Believe me, your day of reckoning will probably start just as soon as this nightmare in this court is over. You all will then ***realize*** and probably ***pay heavily*** for what you did to me on your **'LITTLE ISLAND,'** I mean **STATEN ISLAND.**

Well the Judge repeatedly said **'GET A LAWYER, GET A LAWYER.'** and if I did, the lawyer would have possibly become a part of this sick charade, with you all, this **EVIL BUNCH!** You know full well what part you obviously played and you sure did play your parts well. I serenade you all in the ***DEVIL's*** name, with his permission, and why should you not play the part well? You apparently had the **'Court's Blessing.'** And for this reason, the **Lord** has **ME** in this case on this **STATEN ISLAND** - sorry- **YOU** let these vicious thieves loose on **LITTLE ME.** These insults and your disrespect for me will all be reckoned with ***'en-masse,'*** for this ***vicious gang of liars.***

And the Judge apparently, who went along with this subterfuge with his own little private **'GANG'** of cover ups, well he who plays **GOD** in his courtroom wearing that **DEMON-LOOKING 'Robes of Black,'** will certainly get a ***very special treatment (like roasting in the hell fire)*** for ***aiding*** and ***abetting*** this disgraceful torturing and threatening that I've been subjected to.

When these adversaries, with their very interest in flagrantly subverting the **TRUTH** and the **EVIDENCE**, caused a great commotion, the Judge **THREATENED ME WITH SANCTIONS, NOT THEM. (Boy what a MOVIE this would MAKE.)**

I hope you charlatans – do not think – I am not wise to you, that I am not aware of your ***planning*** and ***plotting,*** through ***your skullduggery and your hateful, sinful, degrading schemes***. I did not miss a trick. Your ***lies*** and ***discourteous treatment*** to me in that obviously **DIRTY LITTLE PIG STY (COURTHOUSE)** gave you away. ***Oh yes, I gave you enough rope to hang yourselves, as a matter of fact, there were so many of you that needed hanging, the rope might have run short.***

Think back to those mornings when I entered the courthouse, ***you all snarled and hissed at me.*** You huddled together planning your *dishonest* and ***treacherous strategies,*** so many of you, against **LITTLE ME. SHAME, SHAME, ON ALL OF YOU!** By your disgusting conduct in that building, ***justice probably has a price, but takes a holiday when honesty is being sought,*** the motto seems reverberating in those cold moldy, insensitive walls. **"Grab what you can, even if it does not belong to you, covet others belongings, others property. Hooray for me, the HELL with you!**

Two people had the keys to **Bernard's** home. It was **RIDDLED,** it was **RANSACKED,** it was **PLUNDERED**……**His Holy Cross** was *ripped* from the walls, and **HEAPED** ***in the middle of the floors along with all the Bureau drawers yanked out. Shirts, clothing, everything was strewn all over the floors, and so much more. His exercise machines*** – **GONE!** ***His valuable Watches and Checkbooks*** - **GONE. WHAT HAPPENED TO THE SAFE HE BOUGHT WITH OVER $25,000.00 IN CASH INSIDE IT?** So many other items I can recall, but are too numerous to mention……..

Yet this leech, this lawyer/Will writer and maker with **ALL KINDS OF ERRORS,** made fantastic immoral billings for so called **'PICKING UP THE MAIL'** daily – for the sum of **$300.00 an hour.** He obviously ***cleaned up,*** and ***cleaned out*** **with those wretched, devious shriveled up heart and hands of his.** It is sickening and heartbreaking to write about the things they had done. I was finally given permission to visit **Bernard's** home after **45 days.** Still I am **SHOCKED** when I remember that scene. To start with, the **TELEVISION** was missing from it's place, and where do you think it went?... **Yes, you are right, you smart people** …. **TO THE ROTTEN, FLESH EATING, VULTURES!!!! (the two-legged kind, that was supposed to protect and uphold the laws for my deceased friend.)** It went **RIGHT INTO THE EXECUTOR'S HOME.** ***(I was*** **TRAUMATIZED** ***when I saw it!!!)***

So I say to all of you possibly ***greedy blood suckers, you leeches,*** it must be a ***disgustingly sick world*** you apparently were ***brought up in,*** and that you ***inhabit.*** You are a ***total disgrace*** to all the ***decent people*** you may come into contact with each and every **DAY!** What a world you possibly live in. What a life you live and what examples you set for your families with you ***cheating, hating and stealing.*** They may be obviously, just like you. ***What an existence!*** **DAY** in and **DAY** out.

I see now how some of you live and treat others. I have the **full picture**. It is quite a dossier about your lifestyle. You certainly set a ***very poor standard*** of the ***doings*** in your **' Small Town Court.'** But I cannot believe that all the people in that Borough conduct their lives in this type of manner. I am so sure you have ***not*** heard the last of **Bernard.** He certainly will come back to ***haunt each and everyone of you and your families,*** for you and yours are sharing in what you may have **STOLEN** from **HIM.** He will **EVEN THE SCORE!**

Bernard appreciated coming out and going to our engagements with us, at least three or four days a week. He did not **SMOKE** or **DRINK** when he was here. He loved our respectable lifestyle and our music and our friends.

Yet, I still cannot believe that the Judge would possibly sign his name to the ***pack of lies*** that his friend, the ***Ex-Judge – now lawyer, probably wrote.*** You just know it was ***a mass cover-up*** by the way they **lied** and **skirted** the issue about **Bernard's drinking**, when questioned on the witness stand. How can this man possibly uphold the position of Judge and still help ***the liars? I am sure, in fact I am positive he obviously made some real BOO BOOS as a lawyer before he became a Judge.*** **I SHALL NEVER FORGIVE HIM**

FOR PUTTING HIS APPARENT SIGNATURE TO THE PUTNAM PAPER, (that he possibly did not compose)~and GOD will not forgive him EITHER!

I believe my part in this fiasco in this court of ill-repute, with its cast of devious partners, has given your **KARMA** a true picture of what has taken place in that building of ***in-justice.*** By the way.....Which one of you broke into **Bernard's** ***house safe and took more than $25,000.00 and his jewelry?*** So **YOU APPARENTLY RAPED his HOUSE, YOU OBVIOUSLY RAPED his SAFE AND YOU OBVIOUSLY RAPED BERNARD**!

Just think if I had a lawyer, **(as the Black Robed One constantly insisted,)** this case would have been over in no time. ***You could have all possibly split the spoils and gone on with your disgustingly shameful lives.*** This is why **GOD** gave me the **fortitude** and the **strength** to see ***this conniving*** you have implicitly done. This is a lesson which is only the start for each of you **AND** your loved ones.

You did this **TO ME** with the possible **'Court's Blessings.'** When I spoke, **you jeered me,** and you ***heckled me.*** The Judge went along with this ridiculous behavior until I asked him to stop you, and only then did he make a feeble attempt to quiet you!

So, when this case is finally over, **THAT** is ***when the real case for you begins.*** **YOU** who have made **HELL on EARTH** for me on this **SLANTED ISLAND,** will now probably get a taste of your own medicine. You will not enjoy what you sold your souls for. The **DEVIL** is **NOW YOUR PARTNER.** Did you realize how you **CHEATED** me and **LIED** to me **UNDER OATH?**

When the Judge made my ***two friends*** leave the courtroom, so you could all do that ***hatchet job*** on me, without the privilege of having any **WITNESSES** around – **GREAT MOVE**, or so you all thought. But **GOD** saw it all. Those names you **CALLED ME,** and all the times **YOU YELLED** at **ME,** and then you even had the nerve ***not*** to allow me to pose my questions. Yes, the **DEVIL** was there instigating you and your **EVIL TONGUES.** The Judge knew I was right, but he was possibly trying to ***'appease his friends.'***

Oddly enough, I rather liked the judge but he was torn between his compatriots who he does his business with **DAY IN** and **DAY OUT!** But this bunch of **HOULIGANS** ran **OUT OF CONTROL,** with possibly **THE JUDGE'S EYES** shut!

As for me, once this is over, I will never set foot on that miserable, self-aiding, dirt bag **ISLAND.** Beside it is one ***disgusting trip*** traveling through that dirty little part of town, to get to the Courthouse. Do you remember the picture, what happened to **Dictator Mussolini** and his friends? **They were hung by their heels upside down in the square in Italy.** Need I say more? Every dictator gets it. They meet their own **WATERLOO!** And **Bernard** too will see what you all have done to **ME, HERE ON SLANTED ISLAND!**

None of you told the truth on the witness stand! In that house that **GREED** built **(courthouse,)** the place where the ***adversaries*** sealed their fate for all time. Because I was seeking the **TRUTH,** all your concealment, to rob me with the possible **condonation** of the court, is to be ***reckoned*** with.

There is probably **no doubt** whose side the Court is on. I bought the **TRANSCRIPT** of that **MARCH 12, 2001.** It sure tells the story. One of the **'Best Investments'** I ever made, ***(no wonder why my friends were put out of the courtroom, so they could not be witness to what these*** **'GOONS,'** *put me through.)*

The **'Black Robed One'** obviously did not want anyone to see what they were free to do with me! So, here I am in this room, with these **lying thieves** and **forgers.** I tell you, ***this transcript is worth a thousand fold more than what I paid for it.***

The **Benched One,** most likely, did ***not*** want my witnesses to observe the show his Brethren put on, and to possibly affirm his biased words and threats that were made to me. **THIS TRANSCRIPT** will show it all!!!

I tell you, it was a most strange and truly frightening experience for me, like being alone in a jungle, with **TIGERS, LIONS AND SNAKES. (I believe I would be more comfortable with them than those in this courtroom.)**

That day in **MARCH the 12th. 2001** was the day of **INFAMY,** the day when the sinners signed on to the **DEVIL'S roster,** for what they did to me from the first day I entered the courtroom, till the end of the case.

ME, who is used to the stage since my first concert at the **tender age of 5** at the **ACADEMY OF MUSIC** on my violin, and all the beautiful performances on stage and T.V. to be in a room **FILLED WITH SO MANY ENEMIES BULGING AND EXUDING WITH AVARICIOUS GREED AND HATE. IT WAS A MOST UNUSUAL EXPERIENCE FOR ME, AND IT WAS TRULY TRAUMATIC!**

The only people I had met were **the Litigants** in this case on **Staten Island.** There must be many wonderful people on Staten Island who are **HONEST** and **RESPECTABLE,** but unfortunately they were not in **THAT COURT.**

YES, THIS WAS MY NIGHTMARE ON YOUR LITTLE ISLAND, THAT DAY ON MARCH 12TH. 2001. THE DAY WHEN THE SURROGATE JUDGE APPARENTLY LET THAT RAMPAGING, RIOTOUS, STEALING MOB LOOSE, TO DO WHATEVER THEIR HEARTS DESIRED IN THIS ,

'TOMB OF HORRORS'

'YOUR HONOR'....WOULD YOU CALL THIS EPISODE....

PREMEDITATED .....

MOB RULE.....

TO SUPPOSEDLY

SUPPRESS.....

MY QUESTIONS??.....

CHAPTER-FIFTEEN

"THE PLOT THICKENS; (WHILE THE MYSTERY GROWS MORE INTENSE)"

The ***EX- Judge*** who sat on the same bench for some ***fifteen years,*** who was called into this Surrogate case by the ***Executor/Will writer/lawyer,*** who made some real fancy **BOO BOOS** in the **TWO WILLS.** The last ***TWO WILLS*****......** ***10 DAYS APART*****,** of our friend, cutting the typist secretary in for 25% ; was asked by the now sitting Judge, "Do you have **Power of Attorney?"** Well when the ***Executor*** said **"I threw it away,"** the Judge said, ***"You better get a lawyer."***

So, enter, the ***Ex-Judge now lawyer;*** he was brought into the case to possibly save the executor's neck, and ,,,,,,...***(other parts.)***

You can imagine my ***surprise*** when I saw the Ex-Judge/lawyer's picture, and it was a **VERY BIG ONE,** dust laden, hanging on the wall, left side of the Judge's bench, in the same courtroom, that he apparently ***'meted'*** out **HIS KIND OF JUSTICE**, for all those many ***tragedy filled years.***

Oh, **YES!** He was ***Mr. Macho,*** **HIS EGO** was as **big as the EMPIRE STATE building,** and he sat on that bench for ***fifteen years probably*** cultivating lies and deceit at the mercy of some poor souls who had to stand before him and address him as, **"YOUR HONOR."**

Still, even without that deadly ***dark*** **Evil Black Robe** attire, he acted as though his apparently ***dirty,***

dishonest rear-end was **STILL** on the ***Bench.*** His ***arrogant attitude*** was positively ***nauseating;*** He did not speak **with You,** he spoke ***at You***.

Well, when I questioned the witnesses that he was engaged for, I was ***shocked.*** He had obviously coached them with such ***precision and dishonesty,*** it showed on their faces.

They were packed with ***lies.*** They were **SO WELL REHEARSED.** It was like watching a ***Broadway show*** in progress. The ***Ex-Judge*** now turned ***lawyer*** for the many **HAT-TED** Ex**ecutor,** put in his bill for rehearsing the Secretary, the Executor and his Wife, the day before **THEY WERE TO BE QUESTIONED BY ME AT THE PUTNAM HEARING.** It was a hefty bill for three hours of him coaching them in **HIS** office, the day before, so their lies on the witness chair were unbelievable. The Judge says the beneficiaries must pay the bill to this Ex-Judge/lawyer **(If this is possibly not a cute pay-off and split.)** Yet, I should not have been surprised with this performance. This was exactly how he probably conducted business as usual, when he wore that **Evil Black Robe** on that Bench where he had ***his bottom safely and serenely planted*** for all those fifteen years.

Oh, if only that **Bench** could **Talk. There was no doubt in my mind of the deals he must have pulled in his day. with that wooden gavel in his hand,** playing **GOD!!!**

So now after several months of his writing his ***heartless, biased*** report **(seven pages)** that the sitting Judge signed ***(there probably is no doubt who wrote it, and no doubt, who signed it.)*** He mysteriously resigned from the case **AND** just as Mysteriously, the wall that hosted his big picture, **LOOKED NAKED,.... SO..... BOTH *the* EX-JUDGE/LAWYER and THE PICTURE** took off....**TOGETHER**.....**RUNNING DOWN THE HALLWAY, AS IF MEPHISTOPHELES WAS CHASING AFTER HIM.....**

NOW TELL ME, WHAT HAPPENED?..... and **WHY?**.....**AND HOW?.....AH, SO THE PLOT THICKENS**.....**THE MYSTERY WIDENS**.....**NO ONE WILL TALK ABOUT IT IN THE COURTHOUSE**, **WHERE SO MANY SKELETONS RESIDE** ..... **DONE IN BY THESE POSSIBLE PURVEYORS OF IN-JUSTICE.**

If our dear Lord brought me into this ***catastrophe,*** I must write about it. This **CANNOT** and **MUST** not, and **WILL** not be shoved under the wooden slats in this **HOSTILE COURTROOM,** along with the rest of the **YEARS OF TEARS** and **DESPAIRING HOPES** by those who sought a **JUST RESOLUTION** to their problem.

I know this has to be the way of separating the **LIARS** and the **CHEATERS** from the **HONEST ONES.** I know for sure their possible retribution is mounting. Believe me, there are no gold stars on their **KARMIC** roster, only **TEARS**, and **TEARS** and more **TEARS** and may it remind them of all the pain they have **caused to all concerned.**

No amount of **GOOD DEEDS** in the future can **WIPE OFF** or **DISSOLVE** all the **HURTS THEY HAVE DONE TO OTHERS…. AND TO ME**.

~AND, I WILL NEVER FORGIVE EACH AND EVERYONE WHO HAVE LIED AND TRICKED, AND PLOTTED, AND DENIED ME THE JUSTICE, THAT EVERY AMERICAN TRULY DESERVES IN OUR COURTS!!!~

~THIS IS OUR AMERICA,…… OUR FOREFATHERS WORKED HARD AND WILLED IT TO US. WHY SHOULD A BAND OF BLACK ROBES DENY US THE HONESTY AND FREEDOM WE ALL DESERVE AND ARE ENTITLED TO?

AGAIN I SAY, THIS IS OUR AMERICA, NOT THEIR AMERICA. NO ONE HAS THE RIGHT TO MANIPULATE AND CHANGE THE LAWS TO ENRICH THEIR OWN POCKETS.

THE COURTS SHOULD BE FOR THE PEOPLE, NOT FOR A HANDFUL OF JUDGES AND LAWYERS WHO POSSIBLY MAKE THEIR LIVING ON OUR SKIN AND BONES.

THE COURT SYSTEM HAS POSSIBLY BEEN CORRUPT FOR SO LONG, IT IS ABOUT TIME THE PEOPLE RISE UP AND LET THEIR VOICES BE HEARD…….. IN UNISOM….. THIS APPARENT INJUSTICE HAS BECOME

COMPLETELY OUT OF HAND.

ANOTHER DAY MUST NOT GO BY THAT THESE ESQUIRES WITH THEIR ATTACHE CASES AND BLACK ROBES CALL THE SHOTS……. WE HAVE WAITED LONG ENOUGH, ………WE HAVE PAID MUCH TOO MUCH…….WHEN WE GO TO COURT SEEKING OUR RIGHTFUL JUSTICE, WE SHOULD NOT BE LEAVING BROKEN-HEARTED, BECAUSE SOME APPARENT DEAL WAS IN THE OFFING.

I PRAY THAT THIS INJUSTICE WILL END SWIFTLY,….. WITH THE LORD'S MERCIFUL INTERVENTION!!!…….

~~~~AMEN!~~~~

CHAPTER SIXTEEN

"THE PURPOSE, THE REASON, THE RESULT!"

I now understand the ***message*** from the ***masters.*** It is ***they*** who wanted me, and projected me, into this case. **THERE ARE NO ACCIDENTS.** It is all **PREDESTINED.** My meeting the great conductor **D'ARTEGA** when I was seventeen, who was my mentor, **(my mother introduced his style of arranging to me an at an early age,)** and **Bernard** coming into my life at this point, and then the whole episode in the court, are all ***mysteriously connected.***

~And the manipulating dubious Executor who has caused this **HOLOCAUST,** who **LIED** and **STOLE** from our friend's (**Bernard's)** home, is the epitome of **DISHONESTY.** His **THIEVERY, <u>will not go unheeded</u>** by the **GOOD LORD!** I see it clearly now, how the Judge and all involved have obviously played their roles in ***this catastrophe.*** This crooked Executor who apparently manipulated **TWO NEW WILLS-TEN DAYS APART** and **FORGED SIGNATURES** of my friend. I engaged a ***handwriting expert*** who studied these documents and said in his affidavit, it was **<u>NOT THE LEGAL SIGNATURE</u>** of **<u>Bernard!</u>**

My being involved in this case and meeting all these people who are my ***adversaries*** have a very special reason and meaning. There is a most ***definite purpose*** for my being in ***this venue.*** It is for me-***the curtain has been lifted*** and the ***fog vanished.*** I see clearly now ***my enlightenment of this court system.***

I am grateful that I was chosen to see this ***disgusting***, this ***lying,*** this ***cheating,*** the ***maneuverings,*** so I could let the public know the goings on in these supposedly ***'Courts of Justice.'*** Ah, yes-and it is truly a ***subterfuge,*** because ***what takes place in the open courtroom, has been obviously well rehearsed in the backrooms, in the Judge's chambers and their well planned phone calls.*** They are all in it, but the **HONEST LITTLE PERSON** who pays his **hard earned dollars,** engages a lawyer to seek his honest and just decree, find themselves thwarted by these **'HOULIGANS!'**

To think you rest your fate in the hands of these ***dubious manipulators,*** the ***lawyers,*** and the ***Judges.*** Dear sweet unknowing readers, do not feel your case was not a good one, because the Judge did not give you an **HONEST DECISION**. He only gave the **LORD** above, more reason to see what **SINS** they have **BROUGHT ONTO THEMSELVES.** For that, they will pay and when they stand before **GOD** and are judged, **WELL,** they will **PAY HEAVILY FOR THOSE DEAL - MAKING DECISIONS!**

TODAY I REALIZED WHY I WAS IN THIS CASE SO THAT THESE PEOPLE WHO STOLE AND LIED COULD SHOW THEIR TRUE COLORS. I WAS MILES AWAY FROM MY HOME IN THIS COURTHOUSE TRYING TO GET THE JUSTICE I DESERVE FOR MY FRIEND, (BERNARD), BUT THE HOSTILITY AND THE TREATMENT I WAS GIVEN BY ALL INVOLVED,

THIS BAND OF ADVERSARIES, HAS ENLIGHTENED ME. I NOW FOUND THE REASON FOR THIS EVENT IN THIS CARNATION FOR ME. I NOW SEE MY PURPOSE AND I FINALLY SEE THE WHOLE THING VERY CLEARLY AND YES... I LEARNED A LOT!

I KNOW THAT THE KARMIC DEBT THAT THESE PERPERTRATORS HAVE BROUGHT ONTO THEMSELVES, ARE POSSIBLY AS EVIL AS EVIL COULD BE....

AND THEY WILL PAY!

YES! .....

ALL I WANTED WAS THE TRUTH-WHICH THEY NEVER GAVE ME!!! BUT THEN AGAIN, WHY SHOULD THEY?.......... THEIR GREED, ...WAS..... SO..... OVERPOWERING......

AND.......

THEY HAD.........

SO MUCH.....

TO COVER UP!.....

CHAPTER SEVENTEEN

"SUPPRESSIONS"

In all my **readings** and ***learning's,*** I have come to ***one conclusion,*** that these ***three thoughts*** will ***haunt*** you for the ***rest of your days***, if you do not let your ***conscience*** be your *guide.* And it is this, the most ***overworked*** phrases;

1. **WHY DIDN'T I?**
2. **IF ONLY I DID.**
3. **I SHOULD HAVE.**

I now ***realize,*** I might ***regret* my silence** concerning the court's Suppression of **Bernard's ALCOHOLISM** revealed by the testifying witness, **Mr. Ernest Lombardi, and totally excluded in the report on** the **PUTNAM HEARING.**

Apparently the final report was written by the former Surrogate Judge who presided for fifteen years in the same courtroom. He now returned as a defense attorney for **Mr. Marraccini,** the **WILL WRITER** with (many hats.) Judge Fusco signed the report!

In May of 1999, **GLORIA PARKER** and Company were engaged to perform at the **Black Forest Restaurant** on **Long Island.** While we were all seated at a lunch break, **BERNARD STOOD UP AND DECLARED, "I WANT YOU ALL TO KNOW THIS: I AM AN ALCOHOLIC** and because of

GLORIA and **ERNIE, I HAVE GIVEN UP DRINKING AND SMOKING AND I HAVE NEVER FELT BETTER. I NOW HAVE SOMETHING TO LIVE FOR."**

Mr. Robert Jarvis, a member of **my musical** ***group deposed*** in his ***affidavit,*** that **Bernard** rose from his ***seat*** at the ***luncheon*** and also addressed ***my musicians.***

Mr. **Ernest Lombardi,** an **ill** but courageous witness, who spent almost every weekend with the deceased **Bernard,** made this two plus hour trip to **STATEN ISLAND** to give the following Exact Testimony:

"I spent ***much time*** with **Bernard.** He l***oved us,*** he ***loved*** the ***music,*** he **loved going** to the ***engagements with us,*** he loved **T.V.** He told me his ***life history;*** how he was an **ALCOHOLIC** and how **MISS PARKER** helped him to stop ***drinking*** and ***smoking."***

Now that testimony by **Mr. Lombardi** won extraordinary commendation by **Judge Fusco; "YOU DID A FINE JOB-YOU WERE THE BEST WITNESS WE HAD TODAY." <u>YET THIS PERTINENT TESTIMONY WAS DELIBERATELY EXCLUDED FROM THE FINAL HEARING REPORT, AS WAS THE IDENTITY OF THIS WITNESS, AT THIS PUTNAM HEARING. WHAT A DISGRACE.....WHAT AN OUT AND OUT LIE TO HAVE OMITTED MR. LOMBARDI'S ACTUAL TESTIMONY, AND BODILY, PHYSICAL ATTENDANCE!</u>**

The style and historical ***development*** of this case is further shown by the ***secretary*** of **Marraccini** who was in a ***ten day period*** after the **2nd. WILL,** was ***suddenly*** and ***mysteriously*** put into a **3rd. WILL** for **25%** of the **Estate!**

She has done ***much*** to ***disrupt*** proceedings by her ***cackling, snickering and chuckling,*** when I was talking in ***the court.*** It is ***only*** when I turn to her and tell her to ***stop,*** does the Judge ***finally remand*** her.

She seems to have had the privilege of immunity in this courtroom, and then I wonder:

1. Why would **Marraccini** ***tolerate*** the ***sloppy performance*** of a secretary in writing wills **#2 and #3 AND LEAVING OUT PROVISIONS #4 IN BOTH OF THOSE WILLS??**

She seems to ***enjoy*** an exalted position in the courtroom. Why did **Mr. Marraccini** tolerate her ***gross incompetence*** in ***omitting the 4th***.**PROVISION IN TWO WILLS**-and to add to her ***confusion;***,….she did not have ***the capability*** of ***proof reading*** her own ***typing,*** or maybe she was ***so pressured*** by the **WILL-WRITER** to make those ***changes*** to the **WILL,** she did not even have the time to check her typing, otherwise she would have ***realized*** she left out the **4th. PROVISION and A NUMERICAL SEQUENCE.**

AND HER ATTUTUDE AND EXALTED POSITION IN THAT COURTHOUSE ON STATEN ISLAND, MAY BE THE ROOT CAUSE OF HER INCLUSION AS A 10 DAY BENEFICIARY. ANOTHER SECRETARY WOULD HAVE BEEN SEVERLY REPRIMANDED BY THE

SURROGATE FOR HER CONDUCT AND NEGLIGENT WILL WRITING, OR, ...IS SHE IMMUNE? IF SO.....

WHY...IS SHE IMMUNE??? AND WHY.....THE SECRECY??? AND WHY.....THE SUPPRESSION???

ONLY THE DEVIL KNOWS!!!

I SOMETIMES WONDER WHAT MAKES A PERSON WANT TO BECOME A LAWYER OR A JUDGE. WHY SHOULD ANOTHER HUMAN BEING HAVE THE POWER TO CONTROL AND MOLD SOMEBODY ELSE'S LIFE? WHO GIVES THEM THE RIGHT? CERTAINLY NOT THOSE BOOKS ON THEIR SHELVES. THEY ARE ONLY THERE TO GUIDE THEM, TO HELP THEM GIVE AN HONEST SOLUTION TO THEIR CLIENT'S PROBLEMS..... BUT, TO USE THOSE BOOKS AS A FARCE AND TWIST AND TURN THE WORDS ON THOSE PAGES TO ENLARGE THEIR WEALTH, BECAUSE THEY ARE GIVEN A SHEEPSKIN DIPLOMA. DOES THAT GIVE THEM THE RIGHT TO SHAPE SOMEONE'S DESTINY UNLESS THEY HAVE THE TRUE SENTIMENT OF THE CASE BEFORE THEM?

TO MAKE UNDUE BILLINGS AND TO PROSPER ON SOMEONE'S PAIN AND ANGUISH, IS WICKED AND IS FIENDISH. WHOSOEVER PARTAKES IN THESE EVIL DEALINGS IS……

PLAYING RIGHT INTO……….

'THE DEVIL'S HANDS.' ……..

……..AND THOSE IN HIGH POSITIONS SHOULD RETHINK THEIR CONSEQENCE FOR VIOLATING THE LAWS AND DERELICTION OF THEIR DUTY TO THEIR OATH WHILE THEY ARE WEARING THEIR BLACK-ROBES.

CHAPTER EIGHTEEN

"THIS IS THE SAGA, OF ONE LITTLE CASE, IN SURROGATE COURT, OR............... THE LAWYER YOU ENGAGE, COULD BE YOUR WORST ENEMY"

If this be your **KARMA,** and it certainly is, you have ***earned*** what you will be ***getting.*** Because, ***everything equals out.*** The ***good*** you do, The ***bad*** you do, it all ***returns*** to you. I am a **Rosicrucian,** as ***Socrates, Galileo, Copernicus, Benjamin Franklin, Dr. Anton Mesmer, and so many others.*** **It is a Highly Regarded Order.**

You, each of you know what part you have played in the ***charade*** of **Bernard's WILL.** I, was only seeking the truth, which till this day, **I NEVER DID GET!**

We gave this man many healthy happy days, weeks, months, and years, with no need or desire to ***smoke, or drink*** **ALCOHOL.** Then for one month, because of the trouble he had with his upstairs tenant, he ***slipped*** and went back to his ***drinking.***

He was ***vulnerable*** and was taken ***cruel advantage of.*** That was the Month of ***January 1999,*** when his attorney possibly drew up those ***several wills,*** made ***changes,*** added the ***attorney's secretary*** **(to the THIRD WILL),** and then had her type **this great masterpiece.** All this in the month of **January** when **Bernard** had the problems with that young new *tenant* that caused him to seek ***refuge*** in the **BOTTLE!**

In February, just one month later, **Bernard** returned to my home, sent me Valentine cards and was **TOTALLY SOBER.** He was completely oblivious of that last month of January, when the lawyer drew **TWO NEW WILLS........ TEN DAYS APART!!!**

He was so happy to come with us to our ***shows*** and ***performances***, our beautiful ***concerts*** with my orchestra and all our friends. He loved music because of his many years he spent with the great conductor, **ALFONSE D'ARTEGA,** who resided in his home with him, after becoming a ***Priest.***

When he came out every weekend, he ate well and enjoyed the country-like surroundings. He had no desire to ***drink*** or ***smoke*** (**as I do not allow either**} at my home. He enjoyed the proper living and atmosphere, and great friendship and caring, that our family and friends shared.

And so, **WE** did our best. Now all you who have allegedly **RAPED** his house, **STOLE** his treasures and are doing your best to try to hurt me, I bequeath you all that you have taken from **Bernard,** and desecrated the **TRUTH** and deliberately **TRICKED ME.**

All I have sought, was **HONESTY** and **JUSTICE.** I look down at you all ***scampering*** around like ***lean hungry starving mice*** that have not eaten in months, *groveling* over the spoils: What a **SICK, SELFISH BUNCH OF SMELLY THIEVES YOU OBVIOUSLY ALL ARE!** Look ***behind*** you, ***walk*** very softly, and don't ***close*** your eyes for a minute, because the **DEVIL** is coming to **GET YOU! BOO HOO!** If I did not see your actions and conduct, I would not believe it, I am positive that from **Bernard's** resting place, ***he***

too is ***watching*** you and is aware of all these ***goings on,*** especially, your **'INSATIABLE GREED'**.....
Well, each and everyone of you have probably earned your **KARMIC** debt ***forever,*** from **THIS**, your ***lifetime,*** right into your next. **DO YOU ALL FEEL THE HEAT? HA! THE FIRE OF HELL IS RIGHT ON YOUR HEELS! CAREFUL...OH NO! I THINK IT'S T O O O LATE! SORRY GUYS!**

You should pray, that **YOUR KARMA**, will be **MORE JUST** to **YOU** ... than **YOU** ... **HAVE BEEN** with me.

THERE IS NO HIDDEN DEED.....

THE LORD KNOWS BEST WHAT PART

YOU HAVE PLAYED

IN THIS MELODRAMA!!!

AND, LEST WE FORGET.....

THE PEN,......

IS MIGHTIER.....

THAN THE SWORD!".....

CHAPTER NINETEEN

"TO ALL-WHO HAVE ENJOYED THEIR ILL GOTTEN GAINS FROM THE ESTATE OF BERNARD"

"GET A LAWYER, GET A LAWYER," It seems to be your ***theme*** song. **Each** and **everyone** of you have said this to me, ***dozens*** and **dozens** of times.

This is ***par*** for the course, and that is why I am including these articles to prove my point in ***not*** getting a ***lawyer***, so he can make deals and **I,** lose my **autonomy. Ah yes,** I've been down this road ***several times,*** and I've paid these ***low class, wood eating*** termites **(THE BARRISTERS)**, handsomely, giving them the **opportunity** to make their ***backroom deals. I vowed*** I would **NEVER, EVER** have dealings with ***poisonous snakes***...**(LAWYERS), that is... NEVER AGAIN.** I don't say all the lawyers are dishonest, only the ones I've dealt with.

The poor unsuspecting **PUBLIC** goes through this turmoil at the mercy of these charlatans who dispense **JUSTICE** at their whim and whimsy **OR, 'WHAT THE PRICE WILL PAY.'**

Yes, I am ***including*** some articles ***(which have*** **nothing to do with me)** yet, these are only the ***tip*** of the **iceberg.** This sick **rampancy,** is going on constantly, only under the guise of ***'Seeking Justice.'*** It is ***sad, a sad joke,*** yes, maybe a ***sick, sick joke*** is a better way to describe it. You see, it was done to me by **MY** lawyers and **some of the Judges** who may have ***conspired*** with them. They all made lots of money and favors with all kinds of ***shenanigans*** and ***dishonesty*** in my ***bona fide cases.***

Dear Lord, let me not spend another day within these ***musty, smelly halls.*** Yes, halls that ***reek*** of possible ***deal making*** all in the **Name of Justice.** You, can have it all…..These walls that cry out for the ***injustices*** that take place in it.

I do not ***envy*** you, you who have to make your **so *called living*** on the backs of **the *poor unsuspecting public,*** in an atmosphere of; ***'Who can outsmart the Other Better.'*** The ***merits*** of a case does not ***count or matter,*** only how can you ***MANIPULATE*** and ***TWIST THE TRUTH.*** To heck you say with what is right. ***Honesty*** takes a ***back seat. Your motto and creed that you live by, 'I've got to win no matter the truth, no matter who is right.'***

Well, thank God ***my endeavor*** is one that brings joy and happiness to my audiences. I must live in the **truth.** I don't want to ***outsmart*** people. ***But, the dealings in the court system is one—If you can pull the right strings, and have the right connections, that is all that matters, and the truth gets sidestepped. Justice is thrown by the wayside.***

"Tell me, do you guys enjoy the **bread** you break at your dinner table? Did you ever think how wrong all **those biased, scheming, low down, prejudiced deals** you were obviously making, hurt **innocent people.?** You did it to the **LIVING ONES** and…**EVEN… THE DEAD ONES! TCH! TCH!** I think, if you all were ***given*** the chance, you would possibly ***gobble*** the ***dead, rotten, decaying flesh*** anyway, so that you can get the ***last piece*** of those ***poor helpless skeletons.*** I think you already did that because your monies apparently were not ***sincerely earned,*** and therefore all the food you bought with your ***unjust earnings*** turned into ***rotten flesh*** inside your ***bellies.*** What ***a tragedy!*** What ***sick*** and ***tortured*** souls you all are. **MAY THE DEVILS BE WITH YOU, FOREVER AND EVER! AMEN!!!**

"GET A LAWYER, GET A LAWYER," It makes me want to **VOMIT.** Yes, each and every one of you, Yes, **YOU,** and **YOU,** and **YOU TOO!!!** You have all said it to me ***over*** and **over** again, **CONSISTENTLY,** as though I was ***deaf, dumb*** and ***foolish.***

Well, I did have ***lawyers*** a while back in some cases. **Anti-trust,** and ***others.*** And yes, they ***double crossed*** **ME.** As soon as we got them, they were taken care of, in many ***lucrative*** ways. I guess it is much easier to get ***paid off*** and drop out without having to work for it,

One set of **lawyers** that we had; they had the ***audacity*** to call me from the **airport.** They asked to speak to my associate, who was a **Harvard Graduate, (law review)** my **manager.** They wanted to apologize for **THE DISHONEST WAY THEY TREATED OUR CASES.** Now***, the Government*** was closing in on them. They had done a most ***illegal deal*** in **TWO OTHER VERY BIG CORPORATIONS CASES.**

They had to leave town in a big rush, to avoid being **picked up** by the **F.B.I.** who would then throw their **lying, cheating, immoral carcasses** into jail. They would have been arrested on ***charges of fraudulence, as they lied to their unsuspecting clients*** about the settlement amounts of their ***class action suit.*** This is the way these ***gilt edge lawyers*** did business. This was their

shtick! In fact, the lawyers advised me to get ***today's New York Times, and read all about it.***

So, they were **fleeing** the country to avoid being ***arrested*** and ***prosecuted (I believe they are down in Hades now doing the Devil's work.)*** **Lying, cheating, aiding and abetting** crooked lawyers and judges, just like themselves. Believe me, our cases were **BIG** and **MOST IMPORTANT** or they would ***not*** have been approached to drop out for **BIG MONEY.**

Oh well, that's it. I have ***not*** said it all but for now I hope you get the ***drift*** of why I do not need a lawyer to ***do me in.*** **Gee!** I could write a song – '**GET A LAWYER, GET A LAWYER.**' Alas, it would be a ***sad song,*** and I do not write **sad songs,** only ***happy songs.***

It is a most ***disgusting world*** you people obviously live in-**DOG EAT DOG!** I forgot, that's what you all **ARE** or ***proved yourselves*** to be by hurting ***innocent people*** and apparently ***stealing*** with your **Trickery, Deceit, Wheeling, Dealing and Plotting** ***Ways.*** What a way to make a living. **SAY, HOW DO YOU SHAVE AND LOOK AT YOUR FACE IN THE MIRROR EACH MORNING?**

Last but not ***least,*** whoever has wronged **Bernard** S. (in his ***One Month,*** his ***Lost month of January 1999,*** when his problems drove him **back to drink.** Those that took ***advantage*** of his condition in any ***manner, shape*** or ***form,*** I am sure that he will, from his ***resting place,*** make some restitution to the **EVIL** ones, because he knows who ***befriended*** him and kept him from ***drinking,*** and those who ***tricked*** him and did all those ***illegal wicked things*** and obviously **RAPED** his home and belongings;

he will take care of **YOU ALL** from his grave.....**HE MUST!**

You who have taken part in this **(and you know who you are,) ARE** to be ***pitied, and then beaten.*** You thought you could outsmart **ME**, well I have news for you-don't for a minute think you can get away with it. I now say: **'Let Go and Let God!'**

We certainly did right by **Bernard,** he enjoyed our music, good clean living, **no drinking,** and **no smoking.** I have ***witnesses*** who were with us, and they will gladly ***testify*** to all of ***these facts.***

I can't wait to get away from this **Stench!** You can ***all wallow*** in it, and you all know what you have been ***hiding*** and ***covering up.*** That is why you gave no answers. **NONE OF YOU!** Not one of **YOU** answered any of my questions. You all have ***covered up*** this nightmare – **TOGETHER!....**

But the way ***destiny*** will have it. **IT WILL** one day come back to ***haunt*** you, and **Bernard** will see to it. He was a religious man, and you who have *ployed* him and ***used*** him when he was **drunk and *raped*** and ***ransacked*** his home, ***stole his T.V. and other items and belongings and threw his religious crosses*** and ***Bibles*** all over the floors. **YOU WILL SEE! YOU WILL SEE!**

I feel sorry for your ***greed*** that has done so much to make you sell your souls. How were you ***raised?*** If you have done this ***once,*** it must be your ***lifestyle.*** How do you live without a conscience? Do you have one?

I guess it must be **Real Serious** when the **Surrogate Judge** asked the lawyer (who drew the ***Three Wills,*** the **LAST TWO WILLS** only **TEN DAYS**

APART, so that he could cut the Secretary in for 25% in the third one) if he had ***power of attorney.*** He said **'YES.'** "The Judge then said, I would ***like to see it,"*** and the **Executive lawyer** said, ***"I threw it away," (brilliant move by the lawyer)*** and then the Surrogate **Judge** said ***"You better get a lawyer."***

So now the lawyer gets a lawyer, and guess who it is? Right you are. **YOU ARE SO SMART!** The lawyer for the Executive lawyer is none other than the ***retired*** Judge from this same court, this same Surrogate Court, who sat on the bench for **many, many** years. If this whole mess obviously does not smell bad. **WOW!** what a story, and they are getting away with it ... **(AS YET.)**

It must be serious if the lawyer had to bring in the **BIG GUNS.** It reminds me of a bunch of **RATS** scampering for cover, **when the lights go on.** However, this is obviously, **ONE BIG MESS!**

I truly think this would make an ***unusual movie*** for ***T.V.*** The Public should be made aware of these goings on in **OUR AMERICAN COURT SYSTEM.** The time is **RIGHT**. The time is **NOW.** The reason they do not and cannot deal with me, is I am here for the **TRUTH.** I do not need a lawyer **to distort** and ***massacre*** it. You see, lawyers are in court all the time with other cases, so they have to play the game and take ***turns*** on ***splitting the spoils.***

They make their own ***rules,*** and I am not part of it. I am an ***outsider.*** I am the ***fly*** in their ***ointment.*** The ***truth*** must ***not*** get in the way. They do it ***their way,*** the ***client*** does ***not*** count.

I remember, not too long ago, overhearing two lawyers talking. They were saying- ***"the judge gave you the last case, now it is my turn."*** You see once a month lawyers, judges and politicians have their private dinners where they plot out their games – You can't go, I can't go, it is a closed secret situation. If some of these private meetings were aired on T.V. for the public, this whole dirty mess would be out, and they would not be so **HIGH**-and **MIGHTY.** The ***public*** is at their **MERCY!**

I will not be pulled into their ***spidery web.*** So when they all say, **(and yes everyone who will not answer my questions) "GET A LAWYER",** it means, we can't do business with you. They deal within their clique. This is the secret that **CANNOT BE TOLD....**

This ***band of thieves*** probably have to cling together. They have to swim along within their dirty tide, and that is why they keep saying, **"GET A LAWYER."**

Take for example some families who experience tragic **KARMA** through ***generations. One by one,*** the family has paid for their ***folly*** and ***meanness,*** right down through **generations.**

Well, that is how it works. The good you do and the bad you do, comes back to you!

Those people involved in the ***court system*** **(lawyers, etc.)** who ***curry favors,*** for the moment, the big ***calculator in the sky*** is **tallying** your record, and, it is later than you think. Somehow when I am hurt by these people, their **KARMA** points in the wrong direction and ***each deed*** is ***registered.***

And, just to point up the type of ***manipulations*** **A La Mode** and ***Shenanigans*** that took place in this case.

When we were getting to the point of ***ending*** it, I called the lawyer for the Public Administrator, to get the date for the ***final day*** before the Judge. He obviously kept ***avoiding*** my calls. The girls in his office kept saying he was not in **(I personally knew when the date was to be anyway. But they were supposed to send it to me.)** Finally the lawyer called me and said, ***a man*** came to my home and said, "No one was there!" In fact, **HE** said ***that man*** came to Long Island **TWO TIMES,** to serve the **Papers** of **Particulars** and **Expenses.** I told the lawyer he could have left it on ***my porch.*** I said, "If we are to be in court on Wednesday, **I Must Have Those Papers** with all the billings and the payouts to study it." He said he would send them by United Parcel **Service** and I would get it on **Saturday.** I did receive them and I studied the **Particulars** which were full of **LIES,** and the ***Dishonest Charges*** and their **Phony Billings.** That is why they **DID NOT** want me to have the ***papers,*** because they figured if I got them ***too late,*** I could not make ***changes,*** which were self serving to them.

Monday morning, the Public Administrators' Lawyer calls, **(he was very close to the Judge, this closed shop 'GANG,' on Staten Island,)** to ask if I ***received*** the ***papers,*** and if I would be ready for Wednesday.

This apparent ***phony cheat*** then adds: "When the Judge calls the case, I will stand right next to you, and if the Judge asks you any questions, I will help you answer them." **(now remember, all that bunch including the lawyer and Judge were against me all this while. I could not imagine why he was being so kind to**

volunteer.) I did not need **HIM** or **ANYONE**, I was doing well on my own all this while.

They evidently did their best to make ***my life miserable*** for the three years, so how come all of a sudden he wanted to be such a help? To gain my ***sympathy,*** he told me he just came from the ***dentist*** and was in ***much pain.***

So **Wednesday** comes, a few cases are called and then our case came up **(now believe me, I managed all this while with no help from these enemies, and all of a sudden, HE wants to befriend me?)**

I stand up, and from nowhere, this **'Good Samaritan'** comes out from ***left field.*** He had ***lied*** to me constantly and now he shoots out before me, almost knocked me down, and says to his **'compatriot, the JUDGE', "Your Honor,** the man came to her house **SEVEN TIMES** on Long Island to serve her the ***citations*** for the ***ending*** of the case, and for her to be present in the court on **Wednesday,** for the ***settlement.***

Dear Readers. **NO ONE** came out to Long Island, **NOT EVEN ONCE, NO NOTE** on my **PORCH, NO BELL RINGING**…I was home every morning. I never received any papers. These ***legalized liars apparently*** had the **nerve** to make that statement, they had ***no proof*** to show that he was even there. It was **an out and out LIE! FALSEHOOD! UNTRUTH!**.....

At this point, I put my hands over my ears, shook my head and looked at that apparently **CROOKED BUNCH OF DISGUSTING LIARS.** The brilliant remark from the **ROBED ONE ON THE BENCH,** was, **"MISS PARKER, I AM SITTING ON THIS**

BENCH TILL 2007 AND YOU CANNOT DO ANYTHING ABOUT GETTING ME OFF IT."

Well, I do not have to tell you what I ***muttered*** under my breath. I still do not know why he made that ***statement.*** And, all of a sudden these **TWO TIMES** that the server **SUPPOSEDLY** came out to my home, became **SEVEN TIMES.**

They were probably hoping I would ***not*** show up and ***not fight*** about the ***trumped up billings,*** that would be ***extracted*** from the ***'Beneficiaries.'***

But I was a few steps ahead of this **BUNGLED BUNCH!** I went to the ***room of records*** where all the ***notices*** are kept, and two weeks prior, I knew the whole situation. I had gotten ***all the dates,*** the ***phony billings*** and ***charges.*** They were afraid I would question it, and I would ***not*** go along with it.

Yes, I was in the ***midst*** of this ***quagmire*** and **intrigue.** I could see through what was going on, that is why they tried to keep everything from me.

After all, I was an outsider, and they are the **DEVIL'S EMISSARIES** here on **EARTH.**

So I say---Their **KARMA** and their **KISMET** will certainly ***reward*** them for their ***dishonesty.*** And if that is what they have done to me, you can imagine what they do to those others, who do not keep ***check*** of them, as I do. These others, **(innocent, decent people)** in their cases, have lawyers who they ***engage,*** and unfortunately they trust them, but they do not know ***how*** their lawyers handle their cases, or how they make deals with the Judges. At least, I know what is ***going on!!!***

I went in as **'Pro Se,'** lawyer for myself, against that possibly whole rotten, disgraceful, hungry mob and that was from the Judge down; **'His Highness'** and his band of **'ALI BABA THIEVES.'**

The Judge most likely condoned all that they did. He probably gave those **'Robbers'** Carte Blanche to rule that day in **HIS COURT,** with his possible **BLESSINGS!!!**

I truly feel, and know, that those who hurt me, these **EVIL ones,** they will, sooner or later, get what is coming to them. I do not have ***any enemies*** from the **past,** they are all **GONE!** They cannot **hurt** me anymore. The **Lord** knows **BEST** how to deal with them.

And now I seem to be attracting a new **slew** in this latest episode. I cannot agree to have **Bernard's WILL** settled without the **true picture.** I do not need the few pennies, it will only make me feel like a **HYPOCRITE!**

......I must <u>KNOW</u> the TRUTH...

... **Why wouldn't any of you <u>TELL ME</u> the TRUTH?**

... Why are you all <u>HIDING</u> the TRUTH?

... Why, are each and everyone of you

<u>COVERING</u> <u>UP</u> the TRUTH?

HOW CAN THESE DEAL MAKERS EVADE THE HONESTY IN THOSE HALLOWED HALLS OF THAT PERSON STANDING BEFORE THEM AND IS NOT GIVEN JUSTICE BECAUSE OF SOME POSSIBLE MACHIEVELLIAN ACT.

THE SPIRIT OF THE LAW IS TO FIND THE TRUTH! MAN IS UNJUST…..BUT GOD IS JUST…..

AND….. FINALLY…..

<u>JUSTICE TRIUMPHS</u>!….

~~~AND <u>THAT</u>............

IS WHAT <u>KARMA</u> IS~~

CHAPTER TWENTY

"WAS IT A DREAM?"

After reading the apparent ***disgustingly biased decision*** of the **Surrogate Court Judge,** who is only sitting for t***wo years,*** I realized that the **Ex-Judge** who has now reverted back to being a *lawyer,* after sitting on that ***very same bench*** in that ***very same courtroom*** for some ***fifteen years,*** was probably the **AUTHOR** of this paper. **YET,** the sitting Judge obviously ***signed*** his name to **this disgraceful, lying, blood-stained decision.**

THESE people of ***the court,*** who <u>**demolish**</u> the <u>**Truth,**</u> because the <u>**Truth**</u> hampers their decision. The <u>**Truth**</u> has no place in their ***neatly biased agendas.*** They have set up their own little <u>**'candy store,'**</u> their own little possibly <u>***private business***</u> in the courthouse, <u>**with *no expenses,* no rent,**</u> a ***business*** solely to eclipse the ***veracity*** of the cases before them.

They ***contrive obvious*** versions to achieve a ***premeditated judgment*** irrespective of the ***evidence.*** This whole sham of their manufactured decisions in favor for themselves and their friends, is **SCANDALOUS.** These ***sins*** which will undoubtedly ***fall back* on their heads and their families. The manipulations of the lives of those poor litigants who came before them seeking justice, (WHAT A JOKE) from these 'Demonic Blooded Black Robed' vicious ones. Ministering their so called HONEST DECISIONS.**

They are obviously <u>**CRIMINALS**</u>**,** who are **LAWLESS, and *are unworthy to breathe the same air the* HONEST PEOPLE *inhale.***

Readers, take a look at this whole scenario and tell me….what is wrong with ***this picture?*** The Ex-Judge who served on that very same bench for ***fifteen years (now turned lawyer, but whose picture still hangs on the wall!)*** is now the ***adversary's lawyer*** in this case. He just happens to be the sitting Judge's, **BEST FRIEND.** Now **HE** coaches the witness, then he apparently composes the seven page **PUTNAM HEARING FIASCO**…..which the sitting Judge puts his name to. Then suddenly ***the picture*** disappears as well as the ***Ex-Judge,*** and another lawyer ***comes in*** and ***stands*** before the ***sitting Judge,*** and said that, ***"the Ex-Judge has resigned from the case, with no reason given."*** **"HOW ABOUT THAT!"**

The words in this ***biased decision*** were so obviously ***massaged*** by this possible ***manipulator*** of ***the truth,*** you could almost hear the ***lying words*** come alive as they were ***uttered*** from their ***dishonest mouths.*** But it does not shock me. I expected it. I was hoping there was a shred of **HONESTY** ***in this court.*** **THIS IS A SAMPLING OF THE KIND OF COURT SESSIONS HE PROBABLY RAN WHEN HE WAS ON THAT SAME BENCH IN HIS EVIL BLACK ROBE.**

Yes, they are possibly the ***epitome of lawlessness,*** and they are in ***violation*** of their ***duty*** and the ***oath*** they took. Their **penalties,** and these are guaranteed to them, and their loved ones, are the provisions for their **probable DAMNATION!**

By inflicting the possible lies and dishonest decisions in **THIS CASE** and possibly not permitting the truth in their courtroom, which is twisted with tears and heartbreak. They have fortified their souls to the, **"PRINCE OF DARKNESS.**

They are **VULTURES.** ***When I am in that courtroom, the heavy air is apparently laden with so much corruption, it permeates the atmosphere. These judicial hypocrites*** are building a likely case against themselves. Nothing goes by the **KARMIC** debt they are possibly acquiring, they will pay heavily for the perpetrations they are doing to me.

I know it, I feel it, I sense it. I am a **Rosicrucian** which is an ancient metaphysical order, older than **the Masons. I was raised with all the beauty and understanding of doing unto others as you would have them do unto you.** It is printed in ***many different languages, all over the world. Galileo, Copernicus, Socrates, Ben Franklin, Dr. Anton Mesmer,*** and many other fine reputable metaphysicians are also, ***notable Rosicrucian.*** I belong to the order for many years.

My ***learning,*** my ***teachings,*** as well as my upbringing, and fine family background has taught me much. I have walked this planet ***many times***, and I know for sure that ***these dishonest ones*** who have hurt ***me***, **WILL SUFFER** for their lies to me.

After one of my awful episodes in **THAT** ***courtroom*** on Staten Island,**(the date was August 10, 2000)** I drove that **long tedious drive** home and retired rather early after saying a little prayer, as I usually do. At about **2:30 A.M.,** I seemed to be awakened by a most ***unusual dream.*** Somehow it was ***so real,*** it was ***a shocker!*** There was an airplane landing in a field which was enveloped in an ***ominous haze.*** **Two Black-hooded and Robed Giant-like figures,** emerged down the gang plank, and headed straight to **THE GROUP** that were apparently so ***cruel*** to me, in the courthouse.

They were all there, ***huddled together*** **(as they always did in the hall of the courthouse.)** They were laughing about the ***lies and tricks*** they put ***me through,*** and how ***the Judge worked it all out for them!*** **Oh yes,** he did give me a ***hard time,*** **- THAT PROBABLY INFURIATING DISHONEST SON OF A WOMAN!** The fact was, that they all pulled together, and the decision was in the **BAG!** So now, this chartered plane came to take them on a **'WELL EARNED VACATION'**, yes, for the great job they all did **against ME**. The **giant-like hooded** ***stewards*** with their ***ghastly black robes*** said, **"STEP UP! YOU ARE ALL** holding up the party." ***One by one,*** they **boarded** the plane. Suddenly, **the last one** to get on said, ***"I really do not want to go, my family is waiting for me." Another voice was heard saying, "Oh, you must come along because of that great job you did on that Pro Se, your name is on the list. You all worked together in the court, and you all deserve this reward of a well earned vacation together*** **–ALL PAID FOR BY THE JUDGE'S DECISION."**

Ah yes, I know only too well how ***very deviously*** and ***dishonestly*** they all pulled together to ***cheat me, to trick*** **me,** and **lie** to me about all the facts. They treated me ***like dirt,*** they **planned,** and they ***plotted*** and they ***lied*** conspicuously, on the witness stand. **Yes,** and this is after they have taken the **oath,** to tell the truth.

So now they were all going together, to enjoy ***the spoils of this judicial farce*** that they put me through in this Surrogate Court, with the **(TWO FORGED WILLS) –** ***written in a ten day period.***

They now were being rewarded for their ***lies*** and the ***parts*** that they all ***played so well.*** So, this trip was probably a ***grand payoff*** for this ***bunch of gangsters,*** and the ***sharing of the 'Loot,' which they stole from me.***

In my 'dream' the ***hooded stewards*** in those **Black Robes** reminded me of those awful sinister ***Black Robes*** on the bench. I heard a voice saying, " ***there is an impressive party for the great job you did on this case, when we land."*** I heard much ***laughter*** and ***mirth*** about how they ***tricked me.*** They did not think that **the Lord** was watching them, but he knew what they were putting me through.

The reservations with their names on it, was read off , then one of the attendants said "You have earned this trip. It is once in a lifetime experience. You will all share it together. You played your parts well in the courthouse and you sure did **SOME JOB** on that **LITTLE LADY** who only wanted the **TRUTH** and **JUSTICE."**

Then the door of the plane closed and it took off. Just then, I remember in my dream seeing this black foggy cloud lifting and this ominous craft circle the field **THREE TIMES.** I said, " **GOOD RIDDANCE, I HOPE NEVER TO SEE YOU ALL AGAIN**," and as I was about to turn away, I heard this **VERY LOUD BANG** that lit up the sky.

The plane exploded in the air after only a minute of take off. This shock in my dream woke me. **I WAS STARTLED.** It seemed to remind me of the astronauts when their capsule exploded. **WHAT A SHOCK!** And **THAT,** was the **reward trip** for those who ***lied,*** and ***stole*** and ***concealed*** the truth and also ***plotted*** against me.

Well it took a long time to try to fall asleep again. When I awakened in the morning, I was still **SHAKING,** it was so real I kept thinking about the dream and about those very ***duplicitous people*** who ***mistreated*** me with their ***'en masse plotting.'*** **YES,** each one did their share to conceal ***the truth*** about the **PHONY – TWO WILLS-** which were **DRAWN UP – TEN DAYS APART!**

They took advantage of our friend, **(Bernard)** because of his **DRUNKEN BINGE,** when he fell off the wagon for that **ONE MONTH** in **JANUARY.** When **Bernard** sobered up, he came back to sobriety for **ELEVEN MONTHS,** before passing away. He **<u>NEVER</u>** mentioned the **WILL CHANGES** or what that **CROOKED LAWYER apparently** had done to him. What he **DID** say was:

"I'VE GOT TO GET AWAY FROM THAT LAWYER – HE IS MONEY HUNGRY. HE CHARGES ME SO MUCH."

WELL, I KNOW HOW POSSIBLY DISHONEST THESE 'LEGAL-ITES' ARE. THEY ARE <u>LEECHES,</u> THEY WILL SUCK YOUR BLOOD DRY AND EMPTY YOUR WALLETS........AND REMOVE ALL THOSE

DEAD PRESIDENTS PICTURES ON

THOSEGREEN BILLS FROM YOUR BILL FOLD.

~ IF ONLY

MY DREAM DOES

COME TRUE! ~

CHAPTER TWENTY-ONE

WHEN I WENT TO BED LAST NIGHT"........

I kept asking, "why am I involved in this nightmare with these lawyers and all, ***concealing the truth?*** And going back and forth to this **STATEN ISLAND** charade, to this **BOROUGH** that I have **never been to before, never ever cared to visit or, to care to spend one minute of my time, in this appendage of New York City?"**

Why have I been **SUBJECTED** to this **HOLOCAUST? Why me GOD?** I never did any hurtful deeds to **ANYONE**, in all my life. Why do I have to be a **RECIPIENT** to this **UNJUSTIFIED,** and not of my doing, **INSULT?**

I meditated long on this question! And then the answer came and it is a **BEAUT**. **WHAT A MOVIE THIS WILL MAKE!!!** People **MUST** believe the **STORY.** What I have **LIVED THRU** as a **PLAINTIFF** here on ***Staten Island's Surrogate Court,*** **YES! YES!**

This intrigue will fascinate the public ***(who*** **ALREADY** *are* very much **AWARE** ***of our*** **'BIASED' Court System.)** It will bring it all out into the open. So many ***have suffered in the courts,*** an example, and it is; of the treatment I have obviously received on Staten Island Surrogate's Court is disgusting. **WHY?** ***Because I am a Pro Se, I would not play 'BALL,'*** or be a **PART** of the possible **CORRUPTION** they are pulling off. I must **OPEN** the **DOORS** and let the **LIGHT** in, and the **STENCH** out!

The public will see the **LIES,** the **DISHONESTY**, the **PHONINESS**, and they will see how Justice or shall we say '**IN-JUSTICE**' thrives in this **SECRET BUSINESS. YES, BUSINESS,** for that is **EXACTLY WHAT IT IS! SECRET! YES SECRET.** ***The Backhanding, Backstabbing, Deal Making,*** that goes on in their ***clandestine meetings, phone calls, cocktail parties, golf outings and, it is happening RIGHT NOW!***

How about my present case, in which I am Plaintiff **Pro-Se?** The Judge asks the self-made Executive lawyer, "Do you have ***The Power of Attorney?"*** The answer he gave was, **"YES."** The Judge then said ***"I would like to see it."*** And the lawyer says **"I THREW IT AWAY!"** At that point the Judge and the lawyer had some words, whereby the Judge now said, '**YOU HAD BETTER GET A LAWYER."**

Well, by now you know who the lawyer is.....yes, the Ex-Judge, now turned lawyer and his very large picture still hangs very high on the wall. **HE OBVIOUSLY SHOULD BE DISQUALIFIED,** at least he should have known better than to **SHOW** up in that **VERY SAME COURTROOM.** But you know these charlatans, they make their own **LAW!** I truly feel it was most **IMPROPER!**

So, there you are. It must be pretty serious if the so called **EXECUTOR** brings in this **BIG GUN,** ***to pull HIS chestnuts of the fire.***

This Ex-Judge apparently has some ego. He talks at you ***(he thinks he is still on the bench.)*** **He sure rehearsed the witnesses. It was disgusting the way they all lied under oath in the witness chair.** He made sure he avoided certain words which I was very well aware of.

Now a movie pertaining to ***this fiasco*** is certainly ***standing room only material,*** and is sorely needed. We would open the **eyes** and the ***doors*** to this ***ungodly system*** – a **system** that helps ***these deal making lawyers*** and those who obviously condone and partake of the spoils, and come out ***smelling like roses.***

Now everyone in this case, and I do mean everyone, and their families have possibly earned a **KARMIC DEBT**, and they are **SURE** to pay for it.

When you do some corrupt deal, when you take the oath, and you lie in front of the flag and the Bible, and you sit in the Witness Chair, you Bought It! **YOU BOUGHT IT MY FRIEND.** The lawyer, the Executor, his wife, his secretary, the Public Administrator and all. They swore ***to tell the truth.*** They **DID** it to **GOD!** They **DID** it to **ME** and the **AMERICAN FLAG,** they **DID** it to the **JUDGE** sitting on the Bench! Let us not forget our dear departed friend, **Bernard,** he must be reckoned with too.

And what they did to **HIS WILL,** and how the Ex-Judge is possibly ***aiding*** and ***abetting*** this concealment, is a **TOTAL DISGRACE!** Our friend, **Bernard,** from his resting place, will see that **JUSTICE** will prevail, ***eventually.***

So, with the treatment I have received on Staten Island's Surrogate Court because of ***this friend of ours who passed away,*** I can only say, **'WOE BE TO YOU DISHONEST ONES.'** ***I was treated so shabbily*** and treated like an ***outsider*** because I was trying to find **JUSTICE.**

I ***was always under the impression that the courts wanted to find out the truth, to know the facts,*** but instead they sweep all the evidence under some ***dirty desk.*** I felt it obviously a most ***hostile place,*** and not one to discover the truth, but to do a good job of ***camouflaging*** it!

They kept insisting **'GET A LAWYER, GET A LAWYER.'** They resented me because they could not do the concealment with me. So, if I had a lawyer, they could make ***deals*** without me and ***wipe me out.*** I must know everything that is going on. **IF I HAD A LAWYER,** I would know **NOTHING!**

I paid good money to engage a **HANDWRITING EXPERT**, a ***Bona Fide*** person with credentials. I also had letters notarized from honest people who knew our friend, **Bernard**, including a statement from each, stating that **Bernard** said – **"HE WAS AN ALCOHOLIC,** and **HAD BEEN SOBER, BECAUSE OF US."**

YET, all this proof is not recognized by this Surrogate Court. **WHY? WHY?** They do not let me put this into the record for evidence. **WHY?** Because they do not want any evidence to come out that would prove this case.....

So, tell me, is this ***not a sick dishonest system?*** **A SYSTEM TO OBVIOUSLY CONCEAL THE TRUTH?** The pals of the court, the cronies who apparently have ***plotted this awful clandestine charade to keep the truth hidden.***

But I know the Lord sees all, and will take care of those who are creating this **HAVOC**, this **NIGHTMARE** on **STATEN ISLAND.** ***These culprits*** are possibly digging ***a hole*** for ***themselves,*** their *loved* *ones* and all, because they are trying to **HURT ME** and **DECEIVE ME!** It will all even out! **GOD** cannot be set **ASIDE.**

We did so much to keep our friend **WELL** and **ALIVE** without the **liquor drinking** and the ***smoking.*** He knows from his resting place and so does the Lord. And so do these ***enemies*** who have done their best with their lies, **to obviously cover up the truth,** and all those who are helping to hide the truth and actual **FACTS**, their **KARMA,** is taking note!!!

~~~AND I WILL NOT FORGIVE THEM~~~
THEY HAVE THE IMPRINT OF THE <u>DEVIL</u> ON THEIR FACES.
~~~BECAUSE OF YOUR ACTIONS, YOU ARE THE MASTER OF YOUR FATE, ALL YOU WHO HAVE LIED AND COMMITTED EVIL. – THEN SO BE IT!!! IT IS TOO LATE TO TURN BACK THE HANDS OF TIME.
~~~AFTER WHAT YOU HAVE DONE TO ME, YOU CANNOT GO TO GOD TO ANSWER ANY OF YOUR PRAYERS,

BECAUSE <u>YOU</u> PUT THE LETTER

<u>'D'</u> ……. BEFORE THE WORD….. <u>EVIL.</u>

~~~AND THE LAWS OF GOD ARE

<u>UNI</u> – <u>VERSAL</u> – <u>LAWS!</u>~~~

CHAPTER TWENTY-TWO

"YOUR HONOR?"

I am writing in my den, and I cannot help but wonder, how do you go home to **your families,** to ***your wives, husbands, children, whatever?*** How can you look at them with ***love*** or ***sympathy*** and make the light of day, when you are asked, **"WHAT KIND OF A DAY HAVE YOU HAD?"**

Do you possibly **RELATE** what went on behind the **LOCKED DOOR OF THE JUDGES CHAMBERS?** The secret **POW-WOWS and probably SICK STRATEGIES** that are being **LAID?** You know full well the poor individual who stands before you waiting to hear the words to an ***unbiased decision, honest appraisal*** that he honestly awaits, that he came before you to mete out your decision.

I then wonder, when you take leave of that courthouse, as you go to your car to go home to your loving family, before you open the door, do you **VOMIT** and shamelessly **PURGE** yourself of that ***disgusting upheaval*** that took place in front of the ***American Flag?*** The obviously ***manipulated decisions*** to accommodate your friends? I can't believe you could become ***so calloused*** to take this all in stride, while being ***caught up*** in ***this spidery web?*** Does it all roll off you by the time you reach your home and are greeted by your family? How do you ***sit down*** and have your dinner? Do you once think of that ***poor human being*** that you ***'insulted in the courtroom today?'***

So again I say, how does a **Judge** feel when he goes to his home after this day? Does he check 'his possibly **TAINTED HEART** of **STONE'** on his bench along with **THAT BLACK SOMBER ROBE?** Does he ever have glaring **NIGHTMARES** of how he conducted the affairs of the day? I'll tell you ***one sure thing*** – if you possibly think you are **God,** and can ***insult*** and abuse another ***human being*** before a full house and an audience in your courtroom, there is something **RADICALLY WRONG**. Today in court, my friend whispered a word to me, me a **Pro Se,** and the Judge ***fell on him*** for no reason **(the Judge was probably burning inside and he had no other way to lash out at me).** Yet , the adversary lawyers can ***talk to each other,*** can ***confer with one another*** and never **get** ***reprimanded*** or ***humiliated.***

Well **IT IS A SIN** to insult a ***kindly innocent man.*** It is a **SERIOUS SIN** to insult someone in public, to make a person ***embarrassed,*** and to ***spill blood.*** How important does it make you feel to have the right to ***wipe the floor*** with ***somebody*** – he did ***nothing wrong,*** only ***whisper something*** in my ear! ….. **GOD DOES NOT LIKE IT** when someone ***shames*** another in ***public.*** Did it make you **feel conspicuously important** in **YOUR BLACK ATTIRE?** When you do not wear the **Devils Color** would you possibly still have the courage to do it? **I WONDER!**

I sit here ***with tears*** in my eyes because of what happened today to someone so kind who travels with me this great distance so early in the morning. Well, **YOUR HONOR,** I feel so sure that the **Lord** is probably giving all on that Little Island ***so much rope*** to ***hang***

themselves, and they ***will immorally hang with their sins into eternity.*** They will all pay for **those dishonest years** that they have caused ***others*** and ***me.*** But….. what happened ***today*** in **YOUR COURTROOM** to my ***friend*** and ***myself,*** they will all answer to a **HIGHER AURTHORITY;** and there will be **NO DEAL MAKING.** You deliriously cannot buy your way **OUT OF PURGATORY!**

They all know they are trying ***to rob me.*** I have only done well for our fellow man and our little animals, and I know for sure, if I am ***the catalyst*** to mystically bring ***these EVIL ones*** to ***their senses,*** they will then know why they are deserving of their **UNPARDONABLE RECOMPENSE, ~YOUR HONOR???~**

~~~AND PLEASE…… REMEMBER

THAT WHEN YOU SIT DOWN

TO YOUR DINNER, TONIGHT

'YOUR HONOR???'~~~

WHILE THOSE YOU POSSIBLY WRONGED IN YOUR COURTROOM TODAY MAY NOT BE ABLE TO HAVE A DINNER, BECAUSE OF THE STRIFE THEY WITNESSED IN THAT ROOM OF HORRORS, WHERE THEIR JUSTICE WAS POSSIBLY SLAUGHTERED FOR A FEW BUCKS THAT WENT INTO A SIDE POCKET.

AND WHOSE POCKET? I QUERY!

CHAPTER TWENTY-THREE

WHO PERMITTED THE TRUTH TO BE MASSACRED?"

I have before me the ***Judge's decision*** in a case where I am the ***Plaintiff*** in the ***Surrogate's Court on Staten Island.*** It is truly the ***most disgusting*** reflection of the kind of ***deception*** that prevails in the **American Court System, that is possibly run by a pack *of Charlatans, loyal to their friends!***

First of all, **THIS DECISION is TOTALLY DEVOID OF THE TRUTH.** The lawyer for the ***Executor,*** the ***Ex-Judge, apparently*** has an ego which is ***bigger*** than the **Empire State Building,** and ***why shouldn't it be?*** He has probably played **'GOD'** on this bench all those years, with his ***'double-dealing.'***

Now, he stands before **the present Judge, of a mere two years who is sitting on HIS HOT BENCH** after all those years. The Ex-Judge, because of his ***seniority and power,*** is unfairly ***distorting*** this actual case even though **HE IS NOT WEARING HIS OMINOUS BLACK ROBE.** But his **BLACK HEART,** whether on the bench or off, the rules are probably treated with ***bias*** in this **UNHOLY COURTROOM.** And this is possibly how they keep this debased foul ***pretense*** alive and well for their ***friends,*** their ***families*** and ***themselves,*** on Staten Island.

Now, this ***Ex-Judge*** who is appearing as lawyer for the Executor lawyer, who did some **DISHONEST DEAL** in this **PROBATE WILL,** has engaged this ***Big High Pressured Gun, to apparently pull his chestnuts***

out of the fire. So you see, the handwriting is on the wall about all of the activity that is taking place here.

Dear Readers, I write about this so you can see just what they have pulled on me. I will **BLAST** this out ***for the whole world to see just how corrupt our Court System truly is.*** I know some of you have gone down a similar road such as this, and ***YOU, ARE NOT ALONE….***

The suppression of the Truth by the Ex-Judge, who coached his witness, and he probably wrote the present two year sitting Judge's decision (**who I originally had respect for)** who signed it, **YES,** his signature is on this paper. **I KNOW IT, I FEEL IT, I AM POSITIVE,** the wording does a hatchet job, on the **DECISION. THIS IS probably CORRUPTION 'A LA MODE' IN SURROGATE'S COURT ON STATEN ISLAND.**

I now know why the **Gods** have me in this case. I am a ***Catalyst,*** **THEY,** each of these ***Judicial bodies*** <u>***have built and are building***</u> their **KARMIC** debt. Not only themselves, but their loved ones will suffer for ***their trumped up subterfuges and misdeeds to me.*** Because of what they are doing in this case to ***hurt me*** and ***lie to me,*** they and their families ***will suffer the consequences of their double dealings.*** Remember, ***everything evens out,*** the Lord sees all, especially this ***one-sided justice*** they hand down. This is ***their style,*** this is ***their practice*** also with others.

They have ***committed*** **a very serious sin,** and thereby **SOLD THEIR SOULS** for ***filthy lucre.*** They have created a ***dishonest*** situation. A wise man once said – **"WHEN YOU DIG A HOLE FOR SOMEONE ELSE, YOU FALL INTO IT YOURSELF."**

I no longer wonder why the sitting Judge let the **SENIOR EX-JUDGE** pull this pretense – this double dealing in the same courtroom. ***I feel sorry for him.*** I thought he was **HONEST,** but ***I guess the pressures were very strong and he succumbed to it.***

So now, they all will pay in God's way. They **INCURRED A SERIOUS DEBT** to **THEIR KARMA**, by probably permitting the Ex-Judge to use the present Judge's name and bench ***to commit this corruption.***

Can you imagine the conversations, the meetings, the double dealings that went on with or without wearing those **DIRTY OMINOUS BLACK ROBES,** that harbor all the **MISDEEDS?** I wonder if they are ever cleaned? ***They should probably be buried in it, with all the Evilness interred with them for all the tears they caused the public who came before them, on their days on the bench.***

All I ever wanted was **HONESTY.** I am only seeking the truth. No one in the court system ever gave it to me - - **NO ONE!** They feverishly avoided the truth, like a plague. The whole thing in **THESE NEGATIVE BUILDINGS** are to **COVER UP** and **MANIPULATE THE FACTS.**

This whole judiciary is built on **FALSEHOODS,** on **GIMMICKS** and **EVASIONS** of **HONESTY.** ***I will say another thing on this situation, all those who knowingly, and criminally massacred the facts in this case, who deliberately swore*** on the Bible, and **YES,** under **OATH,** they will probably **ROT IN HELL FOR ETERNITY.**

Now, what about these **BLACK ROBED CULPRITS** who play God by their misleading deals?

JUST WHAT RIGHT DO THEY HAVE TO TOY WITH THE PEOPLE'S LIVES? Just who are **THESE CORRUPT JUDGES,** and their **SHYSTER LAWYER COMPATRIOTS?** They are the ones who probably feed the Judges these **GOOD CASES in BAD FAITH** so that they **CAN** and **DO SPLIT THE 'SPOILS.'**

Why should these **BENCHED BANDITS** do these deceitful manipulations to innocent people, who put their FAITH in this **UNFAIR SYSTEM?** These **BLACK ROBED ONES** have **NO CONSCIENCE,** they sit there on their **THRONES PLAYING 'GOD'** while little do they realize that God is carefully noting and watching them **DISTORT THE TRUTHS.**

Their day will come sooner than they realize, when they can no longer be in charge of **WRITING** those **ONE SIDED, BIASED DECISIONS,** or possibly sign their name to a **DECISION** that probably some **LAWYER FRIEND OF THEIRS** composed,

I wonder how these Judges will accept the decision from above on their departure from this planet earth? When they are told – **'YOU DO NOT ENTER – YOU DO NOT BELONG HERE BECAUSE OF THE WAY YOU CHEATED THOSE THAT CAME BEFORE YOU,** too many **TEARS** were shed because of your **apparent "CROOKED DECISIONS."**

~~~And lest we forget, the Lord has been keeping score of all the ***false swearing*** and your ***infamous duplicity. Your perjury was seriously noted.*** You will be dealt with what you justly deserve, **'YOUR HONOR.'** This Court System is like a **'SINKING SHIP.'** I want to get as far away as possible from this
~~~

SPOOF of **"GETTING JUSTICE IN THE COURTHOUSE."**

Each time you bring a case, it gives the Judges and the lawyers ***an opening for their corruption.*** Without your **litigations,** they cannot make their ***crooked deals*** and ***favors.*** It is probably one of the **VILEST, MOST VICIOUS PLACES.** And it is condoned by these **BLACK ROBED TRAPPINGS.**

Remember one thing, these **LEGAL-ITES** are probably the **'EMISSARIES OF SATAN,"** and they are here to **SPREAD EVIL ON THIS EARTH.** Oh how they **DISTORT** the facts and the **TRUTHS** in their courtroom - ***that is why they do not allow you to have a tape recorder because you would have proof….***

My life is truly filled with ***beautiful music, kindliness,*** only doing good for others, and to enjoy the bounties of our Lord. This is my background, my upbringing. ***Yet, the court seems to harbor*** **EVILNESS, UNTRUTHS,** and they possibly do it with their **"CROOKED CONCOCTED DECISIONS.'**

FOR THE JUDGE NOT TO ALLOW THE HANDWRITING EXPERT'S REPORT to be introduced as **EVIDENCE** – ***(He threw it back at me.)*** **It** was disgraceful and downright **UNJUST.** My witnesses to the truths spoil their **DEALS.** These prevaricators are **PLOTTERS.** Their **HYPOCRISY, THEIR EVILNESS, THEIR SKULLDUGGERY,** must not be questioned and their avaricious, shameful appetites must be **INTACT.**

Now, do you realize, their wearing of the **EVIL BLACK ROBES** gives them **CARTE NOIR** to do whatever they please! It gives them the assurance to their cronies that a ***'good split'*** is in the offering! **IS THIS NOT BLOOD MONEY??** These so called ***'Monitors of the Law,' who have lied on the witness chair to the questions I asked, under oath, who are robbing me of my rights because of their illicit pay-off.*** Where is their allegiance?

So now you see, the time has come and the time is **NOW**….. That is why I am in this scene, to be the one to possibly bring it out of that **CONTAMINATED COURTROOM OF TAINTED DEALS, DISHONEST JUDGES AND CROOKED LAWYERS.** If I must be the one to unveil this so called, **'JUDICIAL DUPLICITOUS PRIVATE CLUB'**, this closed group with their **BARTERING SECRETS, *I will write and tell about my experiences.*** What they did is **EQUIVALENT TO ROBBERY.** It is **STEALING ON A GRAND SCALE**, and **CONDONED** with **FAVORS** and PAYOFFS.

YES, I AM THEIR CATALYST and you all know who you are. I do not forgive you……**NOT NOW, NOT EVER!** You shall each pay heavily for the **TORTURE** I have endured, the hurts and the disrespect you all have afforded me and heaped upon me in the Courtroom. You are **'BIG TIME GANGSTERS'** not with guns, but with your **'SILLY LITTLE GAVEL!'**

Perhaps I should thank you for this **'NIGHTMARISH' EXPERIENCE.'** You all with your **GREED** and **EVILNESS** did conspire to slay the ***truth*** and ***evidence,*** and what really goes on under those **BLACK ROBES OF INJUSTICE.** I see it all clearly now, you all work feverishly for the **DEVIL,** the real picture is – the **VERACITY OF ANY 'CASE'**

MATTERS NOT! Only **WHO** gets **WHAT, WHO DOES IT** to **WHO** and **HOW MUCH IS MY CUT in THIS DEAL!**

Now all that you **'BRETHREN'** ***(lawyers and Judge's) do on earth, is to propagate and foment Evilness by pitting one against the other.*** Never really trying to bring about a **PEACEFUL, HONEST** solution. The Judges play ball in this **QUAGMIRE OF DISHONESTY** and that is how the **DEVIL'S** game is played.

I now feel sure that the Lord wanted me in this venue, and in turn I shall be rewarded for what you all have put me through. **YOU** and **YOUR LOVED ONES WILL RUE THE DAY YOU INSULTED A LADY— YOU LIED, YOU TORTURED ME AND YOU DISRESPECTED ME ...... SHAME ON YOU.**

~~~AS FOR ME, THIS EXPERIENCE HAS GIVEN ME THE MOST UNBELIEVABLE INSIGHT, OF HOW JUSTICE WAS TRULY MASSACRED, IN SUCH A <u>BIG WAY,</u> ON SUCH A <u>SMALL BOROUGH</u>, ... ON STATEN ISLAND! ~~~

~~~AND HIS PICTURE .... HUNG,

'HIGH ON THE WALL!.~~~

CHAPTER TWENTY-FOUR

"THE DAY WE WERE TO PICK THE JURY; OR THE WRATH OF THE BLACK ROBED DEVILS"

All through this Surrogate case, the Judges' right hand man, chief clerk, was possibly ***the only one that spoke to me civilly.*** So, I felt this would be a good way for me to get ***some of my points across to the Judge.*** Also, it was good for the Judge to know what ***I was thinking.*** You see a **Pro Se,** (attorney for myself,) is **NOT PERMITTED TO CALL THE JUDGE IN HIS CHAMBERS, WHEREAS FOR THE ADVERSARY ATTORNEYS, THEY HAVE PRIVILEGES OF THE 'OPEN DOOR, and CLANDESTINE MEETINGS, and COCKTAIL PARTIES AND DINNERS.'**

Looking back, I believe this 'guy with the **BIG HAMMER**,' relished the **IDEA** of my phone conversations with his chief clerk, and get this: he could find out **what I was saying** and know the **complexion** of my **feelings.** This was my **only way** to get my thoughts across to the, ***'Judge's ear.'***

As the case was prodding along, each side was trying to outsmart me as **Pro Se** – it was mighty exhausting. This **'gang'** from the other side, was constantly ***lying*** and ***cheating.*** Don't forget, I kept it alive for three years, driving them **NUTS!** Then there came a time to pick the Jury. **I HAD TO PAY A GOOD AMOUNT OF MONEY TO THE COURT SO**

I COULD GET A JURY TRIAL, and the court to accommodate this, ***(money which I never got back).***

The Judge's clerk spoke with me saying – **"YOU REALLY DO NOT NEED A JURY, LOOK HOW NICE THE JUDGE HAS BEEN TO YOU LATELY, YOU CAN TRUST HIM."** I guess the Judge must have put the clerk up to get me **NOT** to **ENGAGE** a **JURY, SINCE THE JUDGE PROBABLY DID NOT WANT TO <u>LOSE</u> <u>THE POWER OVER ME, OR THE CASE.</u>**

Dear Readers,…. do you think I could fall for that line? I emphatically said **'NO."** So the day came **WHEN WE WERE TO PICK THE JURY.** I was ushered across the street to an **AUXILLARY BUILDING.** ***My two friends who accompanied me when we went to court, also knew this case inside out, and all that was taking place in this*** **'HOUSE OF HORRORS AND ILL- REPUTE' (courthouse.)** **<u>THEY</u>** - were **NOT PERMITTED** to **WITNESS** this shall we say, **'FIASCO,'** in this miserable **'DE-SENSITIZED'** arena.

So, **THEY WERE NOT PRESENT** at ***this meeting, and they were sent down the hall to wait in a room. I was taken into a very small office. I sat down and another little Judge said he was going to*** **PREPARE** me for the **CHOOSING OF THE JURY.** He asked me **WHAT I WAS GOING TO SAY TO THE JURY** about the case, and to explain **WHY, I** ***was in this case.***

Now, picture this---there I was seated in this small room with all these enemies (Executor, his Secretary, the Public Administrator and his lawyer, and

the Attorney for the next door neighbor.) There were many other people present also, such as office workers, secretaries etc, who were all watching me quizzically as to what was going on. **YET, MY TWO FRIENDS, WHO HAD BEEN WITH ME THROUGHOUT THE CASE, WERE NOT ALLOWED TO BE PRESENT TO WITNESS WHAT WAS ABOUT TO HAPPEN.**

You can just imagine how I felt sitting there, ***(I was the only one besides this little Judge also sitting, everyone else was standing.)*** **I HAD NOT A FRIEND IN SIGHT.** I was **SURROUNDED BY ONE ENEMY AFTER ANOTHER. ME, WITH NO WITNESSES TO CORROBORATE THIS TRUMPED UP treatment that I was about to receive in this 'KANGAROO COURT.'**

I sat there quietly with that ***gang*** who showed ***their true colors*** early on, literally. They were all **standing around me hovering over me, breathing down the back of my neck, and me… all alone, with no friends,** in that little **'ROOM OF HORRORS'…..**

Now, being a show person on stage and T.V. all of my life **(since I was three years old,)** I regarded this as a scene in a movie. I sat there calmly, with my attaché case on my lap, as ***this little guy, who was a retired Judge,*** was given this type of job, so he could earn a few bucks off the bench. He then asked me – **"What are going to say to the jury?'** I said **"I will tell them the TRUTH** - how I met **Bernard** through ***Alphonse D'Artega because this great conductor was my mentor and idol,*** when I was growing up and studying music and arranging, and that **Bernard** met him when he went to Priest School to study for the Priesthood.

However, **Bernard** dropped out as a **'Brother,'** after several years. When the conductor, **D'Artega** became a priest, he came to stay at **Bernard's** home. ***By the way, this famous Maestro, was a very prominent musician and songwriter, with the New York Philharmonic, in Rome, in Milan, in London, and also the N.B.C. Symphony Orchestra.*** He wrote many musical compositions, including the famous **'In the Blue of Evening.' D'Artega** also had written the music for the **PADRE PIO FILM IN ITALY**.

So, ….. when I saw **D'Artega's** name in our musicians directory ***(each year we receive a new one from our local 802 Musicians Union.)*** I was so excited. My mother, a great musician, who played violin with the Lucky Strike Hit Parade Orchestra, had met him too, and she suggested I phone him. Well, I called that phone number many times, hoping to speak with this great conductor, but no one answered.

Finally, one day when I called, someone did pick up the phone and I said – ***"I would like to speak with Mr. D'Artega, please."*** The voice was **SAD** and he said – **"Who are you, why are you calling?"** I told him about the time I met **D'Artega** and the great influence he had with my music. Then he said – **"D'Artega** passed away several months ago." I screamed, I could not believe it. At long last I thought I would finally speak with this inspiring conductor, who was my mentor.

A month went by, and I called again. We spoke and the gentleman told me he had many of **D'Artega's** records and arrangements. He said they made **A VERY IMPORTANT C.D.** and they had been going to all the Radio and T.V. stations promoting it and selling it. The

C.D. was an unusual story written by **Bernard,** with the **music** of the **Great D'Artega,** depicting the story of an **ALCOHOLIC.**

Bernard said he would come to my home and bring some of **D'Artega's records** and songs and **'THIS C.D.'** The story on this recording was **SHOCKING ENOUGH TO MAKE ME AWARE OF BERNARD'S ALCOHOL PROBLEM.** It was **BERNARD'S WORDS** set to **D'ARTEGA'S ORCHESTRA. THE STORY WAS ABOUT ALCOHOLISM!!!**

When he came out and we played it, I was thrilled with **D'Artega's music** and that story by **Bernard,** who narrated the whole thing. At the end of this recording, **Bernard** said – '**LADIES** and **GENTLEMEN**, the story you just heard is a **TRUE STORY. I AM THAT PERSON ON THIS C.D.".…**

BERNARD TOLD ME HE AND D'ARTEGA MADE THIS RECORDING BECAUSE THEY WANTED TO HELP PEOPLE COME TO GRIPS WITH THE PROBLEMS ASSOCIATED WITH ALCOHOLISM. HE SAID THEY SYMPATHIZE WITH PEOPLE, ALL OVER THE WORLD, ..WHO ARE FACED WITH THIS PROBLEM THAT DESTROYS FAMILIES AND HOMES. AT THE END OF THE C.D. HE SAYS TO THE AUDIENCE, " MY NAME IS BERNARD, I AM AN ALCOHOLIC, AND I BELONG TO AA."

Now, getting back to the court picking a jury, here I am sitting in this **'LION'S DEN'**, with this **'GANG OF ENEMIES.'** I said, "**BERNARD ENJOYED COMING TO OUR CONCERTS AND**

ENGAGEMENTS WITH MY ORCHESTRA AND MY MANAGER, - ERNIE. HE SAID HE FELT THAT D'ARTEGA WAS STILL ALIVE BEING AROUND ALL THE SOUNDS OF MUSIC." He did NOT SMOKE or DRINK on **THOSE** weekends when he came out to my home. I am allergic to smoke as are my Parrots and birds. I do not want to subject them to it.

Now picture this – this little Judge said to me, **"REMEMBER YOU ARE NOT TO SAY TO THE JURY THAT BERNARD WAS AN ALCOHOLIC."** I then said, **"WHY CAN'T I, IT IS THE TRUTH!!"** And this **SECRETARY,** who **CUT HERSELF** into **the 2nd. And 3rd. WILLS for 25%,** snickered at **ME** and said **"HOW CAN YOU PROVE IT - BERNARD IS DEAD, YOU CAN'T HEAR HIM SAY IT."** ***(Now, this is the secretary,)*** the **PARA LEGAL WHO TYPED THESE TWO WILLS. The 2nd. was done on January 19th. and the 3rd. was done on January 29th. – TEN DAYS APART! She cut herself in for 25% of the WILL and she left off PROVISION #4 BOTH TIMES! THIS CONTRIVED WILL HAD TAKEN OUT BERNARD'S CHURCH IN BROOKLYN. This Provision #4 whereby Bernard WANTED HIS HOUSE ON STATEN ISLAND TO GO TO HIS CHURCH IN BROOKLYN. IT WAS IN THE 1ST. WILL** but was **MISSING IN THE 2ND. AND 3RD. WILL AND ALL OF A SUDDEN, THE SECRETARY IS IN FOR 25% CUT?** How do you type **TWO WILLS** leaving **Provision #4 OUT? It read #1,.....#2.....#3.....#5..... HOW COULD THE JUDGE GO ALONG WITH THIS ERROR???? DOESN'T ANYONE PROOF READ THESE**

WILLS? Bernard was sick when the 2nd. And 3rd. WILLS were made. <u>WHO FORGED HIS SIGNATURE</u>??? (THE HANDWRITING EXPERT who I engaged said it was <u>NOT BERNARD'S SIGNATURE</u>!) BERNARD HAD <u>WILLED</u> HIS <u>HOUSE TO HIS CHURCH IN BROOKLYN.</u> HIS WHOLE FAMILY WAS BURIED FROM THERE. HIS DAD, HIS MOTHER, SISTER, BROTHER, AND WIFE. BERNARD ALSO WANTED HIS FUNERAL SERVICE TO TAKE PLACE FROM <u>THAT</u> CHURCH (WHICH WAS <u>ALSO STATED</u> IN <u>PROVISION #4</u>), however, the **SERVICES** were held in **<u>ANOTHER</u> CHURCH** on Staten Island, **<u>AGAINST HIS WILLED WISHES.</u>**

They had a **<u>'FOR SALE'</u>** sign out in front of **Bernard's** house. **I was the <u>ONLY ONE TRYING</u> TO <u>FIND JUSTICE,</u> AND ALL OF THEM WERE JUST 'THWARTING' IT, AND ME. I PLEADED WITH THE JUDGE TO REMOVE, THE 'FOR SALE' SIGN FROM THE HOUSE, SINCE BERNARD'S WISHES WERE FOR THE HOUSE TO GO TO HIS CHURCH. BUT ALAS!.... <u>NO</u> <u>ONE</u> WOULD LISTEN TO ME….. MY WORDS FELL ON <u>DEAF EARS.</u>**

BERNARD WAS THE LAST MEMBER IN HIS FAMILY. The **EXECUTOR KNEW <u>NO</u> ONE <u>WOULD</u> <u>QUESTION</u> HIS CONIVING ACTIONS AND THIEVERY. AFTER ALL, WHO WOULD KNOW THE DIFFERENCE - RIGHT? BUT HE DID NOT KNOW ABOUT <u>ME</u>,… THE PERSON WHO WAS GOING TO THROW A WRENCH INTO THE WORKS,….. <u>THE PRO SE</u>….. FROM**

LONG ISLAND WITH STAMINA AND FORTITUDE TO STAND UP AGAINST THOSE POSSIBLE GLUTTONOUS VERMON.....THIS IS WHY THEY ALL HATED ME!!!

Now getting back to the jury selecting, I opened up my attaché case and **SHOWED THEM THE CASSETTE** with **Bernard's** voice saying **He Is An Alcoholic,** etc. **I WAS TOLD I MUST NOT SAY THAT WORD – ALCOHOLIC! So I said,.... 'WHY CAN'T I SAY IT, IT IS THE TRUTH.'**

After some haggling, I was **THREATENED NOT** to say that word –**'ALCOHOLIC!'--**

We finally were moved into the jury room and was seated at this long table with the jury candidates facing us. I sat at the right end of the table and the little Judge sat to my right, towards the front. So, the scene is now changed; The Executor, the Administrator, and each one had the opportunity to address the jury and **TELL THEM WHAT KIND OF A CASE THIS IS, AND THEN IT CAME TO MY TURN.**

I explained my musical background and how I met **Bernard** and of course about **D'Artega.** I mentioned about the girl's band I was conducting and how the Drummer came down from the 3rd tier to sing – **'In the Blue of the Evening,' (D'Artega's song)** and how I jumped up to the drums. The Judge seated at my right, sat with his left arm over the back of his chair, enjoying my talk and smiling. Well, give me a captive audience and I am in business. **THEY WERE ALL SO VERY INTERESTED IN MY STORY.** Then I started to tell them that **Bernard** could not come out that weekend because of the great snow storm we were having, and travel would be bad and hazardous, so he stayed home.

Well, Friday evening when I called him to see how he was, his voice was **'GARBLED'.** He asked who it was, as he did not recognize my voice. He was **'INEBRIATED'**, he had fallen off the wagon – **HE.. WAS… DRUNK!**

WELL….YOU JUST HAD TO BE THERE TO SEE WHAT TOOK PLACE IN THAT ROOM!!! These adversaries went **BALLISTIC!** The Proverbial **'S..T'** hit the fan! They were **FURIOUS…. THEIR FACES WERE RED WITH ANGER, AND PANDEMONIUM TOOK OVER AT THIS LONG TABLE ALL BECAUSE I SLIPPED, AND SAID 'THAT WORD' (Alcoholism)** …. **THEY DISMISSED THE JURY IN A FLASH!**

At that point they had meetings by themselves, and refused to let me in on it. They did not know what to do with me. They were saying if they pick another jury, she will slip again – this is what was being discussed in my absence. **TELL ME, WHY OH WHY WERE THEY SO AFRAID TO LET THE TRUTH ABOUT BERNARD'S ALCOHOLISM COME OUT IN THE OPEN?** Well they made me promise **I WOULD BE MORE CAREFUL, AND NOT SAY THAT WORD, 'ALCOHOLISM.'**

So they finally get another group together for the jury. By this time, it was getting more difficult for them to find people to pick for the jury, because there were not too many prospective jurors left to choose from.

Once again, we took the same seats as before at the long table with this little judge to my right, all facing a new audience. **AGAIN EVERYONE GAVE THEIR LYING CRAPPY SPEECH** about the case, and **NOW IT WAS MY TURN.**

I DID GREAT! I told them how I met **Bernard** through **D'Artega,** and **Joe Glazer, the Big Impresario** brought **D'Artega** to write the arrangements for my orchestra with me conducting this group. **D'Artega** built this whole show around me and my instruments. And how I played, **'In the Blue of the Evening,'** on the Marimba. At this point, everything was going fine. The little Judge seemed so pleased and engrossed in what I was saying. **HIS FACE** had a smile and seemed to enjoy me talking about my music and show business. My adversaries were sitting on the tips of their chairs, anxiously awaiting for me to end my little talk. Every now and then I turned to look at the expressions on their faces. I was amused by their **'DOUR EXPRESSIONS.'** I couldn't help but think to myself…they looked like a bunch of drowning **RATS. If only I had taken along my camera** to snap that **PICTURE. AND WHAT A PICTURE THAT WOULD HAVE MADE, BECAUSE AT THAT POINT, I WAS SO ABSORBED IN TELLING THE STORY AND EVERYONE OUT FRONT WERE SO INTERESTED IN LISTENING TO WHAT I WAS RELATING,….YES LADIES AND GENTLEMEN, I MADE….THAT….. PROVERBIAL SLIP, WHEN I STARTED WITH THAT SENTENCE …. "WE HAD A SNOWSTORM AND BERNARD COULD NOT COME TO LONG ISLAND BECAUSE IT WAS TREACHEROUS AND HE HAD TO STAY HOME.." I CONTINUED BY SAYING HOW I**

CALLED BERNARD THAT EVENING AND HOW HE DID NOT RECOGNIZE MY VOICE. HE ASKED .. "WHO IS IT?" I COULDN'T BELIEVE IT – BERNARD WAS HIGH.... HE FELL OFF THE WAGON!!!

Need I tell you more.....that at this juncture, **MAYHEM** took place in that room. I could not help it, I got caught up in telling my story so, **THAT'S HOW I SLIPPED** about **ALCOHOL! POW! WOW! XZXZXZ...THEIR EYES WERE ABLAZE WITH ANGER** That did it! By this time, they were totally **DISGUSTED.** There were not too many jurors left to pick from and so they thought anyway she would slip again. And, of course, they were **NOT TOO ENAMORED WITH ME FROM THE START.**

To add to this delightful misery, it was the day the heavens opened up to herald this **JURY PICKING DISASTER.** It was almost time to break for lunch. **IT WAS A MIRACLE THAT THEY STILL HAD SOME KIND OF AN APPETITE FOR FOOD AFTER THE MORNING THEY HAD WITH ME.** I decided to have some orange juice from the juice machines, in the alcove room. My friends wanted to bring me back a sandwich or something, but I declined **(the restaurants around the court were awful.)**

These possible **DECEIVERS** who circumvent the truths with their **DECEPTIONS,** all went out to lunch, but I stayed back. Before they left, the **LAWYER for the PUBLIC ADMINISTRATOR TOOK ME ASIDE AND PRACTICALLY THREATENED ME.** He said – "Everybody is very mad with you because you are holding up this case. **NOW IF IT DOES NOT GET**

SETTLED, ALL OF BERNARD'S MONEY WILL GO TO THE GOVERNMENT, AND THE BENEFICIARIES WILL GET NOTHING! THEY WILL BLAME YOU!" Then they all left for lunch.

So I sat in this anti-room alone, sipping my orange juice. Some time later, the apparent, **'SUPPRESSING OF THE TRUTH GANG,'** returned from their lunch and had a **SECRET MEETING WITH THE JUDGE**. The little Jury Judge came over to me and said, "The Judge in this case wants you to come over to the main courthouse. He has something to tell you **(I guess their lunchtime was spent with the main Judge too!)** They told him **THEY CANNOT HANDLE THE ORDEAL WITH ME.** In other words **I HAD THEIR NUMBER AND I WAS IMPOSSIBLE!!!**

This probable **GROVELING GROUP OF VULTURES,** stared at me. After all **WHO AM I** to come into **THEIR COURT AND EXPECT AN HONEST CASE AND DECISION? I MESSED UP THEIR BUSINESS IN THEIR COURTROOM.** This whole bunch were contemptible and very possibly untrustworthy.

The trip to Staten Island for **THREE YEARS,** to that courthouse, was by this time, **ENOUGH FOR ME.** I saw how the Law was being slaughtered, and how these 'legal-ites' earn their monies. This is their lifestyle. It must be most disgusting to do this everyday of their existence in this system.

I finally agreed to settle this case **AFTER HOLDING OUT FOR MORE THAN THEY WANTED TO GIVE ME. THEY SURE WANTED**

THIS FIASCO TO BE OVER, SO THEY GAVE ME PRETTY MUCH OF WHAT I WANTED. ***But I never found out the who stole all the money out of Bernard's home safe (with the hole in it,) and who stole all of the items from his house..***

The secretary ***was crying*** because she had to give up a percentage of **HER TAKE.** ***The many hat-ted Executor*** also had to give up something. I can just see the bunch doing their business as usual to those other litigants on Staten Island.

It sure is great ***not*** to go into that courthouse where the **'DEVIL'** sits, taking notes of the compatriots that will be **INMATES, IN THE NEAR FUTURE** in his **LAIR IN HELL!** I also heard the Judge had triple heart by pass surgery when the case was finally over. I still have the papers he signed **HIS** name to, with the lies that his friend, the Ex-Judge , composed in the **'PUTNAM HEARING!' WHAT A DISGRACE.** These animals should be hung by their.......**TAILS!**.

And these are some of the traumatic experiences with lawyers and Judges, without conscience, who are **PHONIES.** For a sum of money, about **$50,000.00,** one can become a Judge, and rake in the hoards of ' **DEAD PRESIDENTS ON GREEN PAPER,'** such as **Grant, Franklin, Washington etc. AND FOR THAT, THEY SELL THEIR ETERNAL SOULS.**

So, once their bottom hits that bench, they want to get a piece of the **ACTION!** They go for **BROKE!**

I happened to pass a room **(chambers)** one day and the yelling could be heard outside in the hall. The

Judge was heard saying **"I gave the decision to you on the last case, I have to give it to him this time."**

Now you can see, ***literally, you take your life in your hands when you go into court.*** It starts the ball rolling the minute you engage a lawyer. They **CHARGE** you by the **MINUTE,** the **HOUR,** etc. How in heavens name do you ***really know what he is doing or the hours he is putting into your case,*** or if he is busy on another case or maybe tickling his girlfriend! If you call these 'shysters,' ***on the telephone, they charge you for the time too.***

And this is like that from **Top to Bottom.** Most of these lawyers are unscrupulous and **EVERY JUDGE WAS A LAWYER BEFORE HE BECAME ONE OF THESE 'MUTINEERS OF JUSTICE.'**

They are probably a disgrace to the **'HUMAN RACE.'** They hold the title of **'MANEUVERING CONTRIVERS.'** They consider themselves **'BROTHERS ON THE BENCH' – YES THEY ARE BROTHERS - THEY ARE THE ORIGINAL CAIN AND ABEL, BROTHERS IN CRIME!**

On *that Bench of Wood, they are 'Demons Possessed with Power!* Can you imagine another human being addressing them as **'YOUR HONOR?' They** are **NOT GOD.** They think they are, but they should remember they are not without the curse of those to whom they have given a wrong decision, so they could probably be **PAID OFF** by the guy he so **REWARDED.**

I am so aware of these heartless **'BEDEVILLED BLACK ROBE' wearers.** I truly feel I was chosen to suffer by the hands of these **'MEN OF DARKNESS.'** I am bringing this out into the open by writing this book, and recording my C.D. which I both wrote and sang , and recorded along with my orchestra. The name of my **C.D.** is **CORRUPTION REIGNS IN THE COURTROOM……**

With my fine background and family, I would much rather write about beautiful things – songs, lyrics, poetry etc. But I was so disgusted with my experiences with these '**SELF SERVING DECISION MAKERS,**' that I had to put pen to paper to alert you. Dear Readers, please, keep your eyes and ears open when you **DEAL** with these **LAWYERS AND JUDGES**.

The courts that I have had the displeasure of bringing my various actions were - **FEDERAL COURT IN UNIONDALE, NASSAU COUNTY N.Y., FEDERAL COURT IN HAUPPAUGE, SUFFOLK COUNTY, N.Y., FEDERAL COURT IN FOLEY SQUARE, NEW YORK CITY, AND THE SURROGATE COURT ON STATEN ISLAND, N.Y.**

Being a plaintiff and not (shall we say) '**IN WITH THE JUDGES,**' it was ***not*** a ***'field day or picnic'*** for me, as a **Pro Se.** Some of these lawyers I retained were on '**BOTH SIDES OF THE FENCE**' playing ball with the other side -- lawyers and the Judges and ***<u>Taking my Money!</u>***

This law business is an <u>Experience,</u> a <u>Nightmare,</u> a <u>Curse</u>. You do not know what is going on behind your back, in the Judges chambers in the ex-parte meetings. Only the **DEVIL,** is 'plying' these Esquires. He is giving them enough rope so they can insure the trip **DOWNWARD,** to the Bowels of the Earth, where their earthly conduct has provided them with this **BOTTOMLESS PIT!!**

And ….. ***There they will learn the pain and the suffering that their Biased Paid Off Decisions, that they gave to those poor litigants, who addressed them as*** **'YOUR HONOR!'** It is **THEN** that the bitterness and suffering, the agony that they inflicted on others from their **UN-HOLY BENCH** will plague and haunt them for Eternity with none other than the **'DEVIL,'** himself.

They played the game of chance with their wooden gavel. Whichever lawyer or friend gave them a better cut or deal, that was the one that got the favorable decision. Like that **Judge Garson in Brooklyn,** who **sold his soul** for some **fancy cigars,** and other **appetizing teasers.** Those **'MEN IN BLACK'** with their scepters, **(gavel)** of **AUTHORITY,** who used their **Bench and Robe,** as a wedge to accumulate the Bounty that they will unfortunately leave behind, when they arrive at the Escalator that says, **'THIS WAY DOWN!'**

At some point, do they not wonder that their actions in court would bring about the thought that they would have to pay for their crimes? What makes them any different than the criminals who have been incarcerated for **theft, perjury, forgery, ALL OF WHICH HAVE TAKEN PLACE AGAINST ME IN THIS CASE.**

I have spoken to people and friends who told me of the suicides, and one in particular - of her son – a professional man. The Judge plagued him into this catastrophe where he took his own life because of a biased decision made by the Judge. His mother, till

this day, still writes to magazines and flyers of the biased proceedings that caused her sons death.

So, **these failures to the human race** in their Robes of Evil, who promote the patronage of dishonesty and contribute to the unnecessary hardship of many good families. ***They have possibly caused the downfall and the ruination and the DISRESPECT TOWARDS THE JUDICIARY SYSTEM, HERE IN AMERICA*** because of their, '**BIASED PAID FOR DECISIONS.**'

I will never forgive those corrupt Judges who were the possible **VAMPIRES** in my **FOUR CASES,** and God will have no part of them! **MEPHISTOPHELES** already had his bid in for them. Then, will they get the reciprocation, and retribution for the upheaval they have fomented here on earth. It will be the delayed '**BOOMERANG**' and the '**RETALIATION.**'

Dear Readers, I could go on indefinitely ….. People who have heard my **C.D.** call me constantly, telling me of their unfortunate stories. The ***Endless money sucking Barristers and Judges- THE SADDEST PART OF ALL IS THAT WE HAVE TO ADDRESS THEM AS, 'YOUR HONOR.'***

These lawyers and Judges will never forget the '**LITTLE BLOND PRO SE.**' Our Lord gave me the ***intelligence and fortitude*** to see through the suffering of this, '**NIGHTMARE ON STATEN ISLAND.**' And let us not forget '**MEPHISTOPHELES**' whose Brimstones are never quenched, and these ghouls who manipulate and contrive their own rules in their '**DIRTY LITTLE PRIVATE COURTHOUSE,' who probably** feast on the dead carcasses in this Surrogate Courthouse.

I FEEL SO SORRY FOR ALL THOSE PEOPLE WHO ARE AT THE MERCY OF THESE DECISION MAKERS WHO BLATANTLY HAVE NO REAL INTEREST IN THE OUTCOME OF THEIR CASE, BUT ONLY IN WHAT THEIR PROFIT WILL BE. IT IS RARE TO FIND SOMEONE WHO IS TRULY ABOVE REPROACH, AND WHO REALLY HAS YOUR INTEREST AT HEART.....NOT HOW LONG HE CAN DRAG OUT YOUR CASE TO FILL HIS COFFERS. WHY CAN'T WE BE HELPFUL TO ONE ANOTHER. AFTER ALL, THIS VOYAGE ON PLANET EARTH IS SUCH A SHORT ONE. LET US BE PLEASANT, LET US BE HELPFUL, LET US BE HONEST TO EVERY LIVING SOUL.

WHEN MAKING A DEAL, LET US NOT WALK AWAY FEELING LIKE WE TOOK ADVANTAGE OF THE OTHER. LET US ALL FEEL WE MADE AN HONEST DEAL, THAT LEAVES BOTH PARTIES FEELING SATISFIED.

SOME HUMAN BEINGS HAVE MET THEIR FATE BECAUSE OF THEIR DISHONESTY AND GREED.

THEY HAVE ROBBED AND CHEATED SO MANY INNOCENT PEOPLE WHO TRUSTED THEIR LIFE'S EARNINGS TO THESE BIG CORPORATE HEADS. THEY WOULD RATHER

BUY BOATS AND SPEND OTHERS MONEY ON VILE PLEASURES WHILE TAKING THE BREAD AND SHELTER FROM THOSE WHO INVESTED THEIR HARD EARNED DOLLARS WITH THESE DOWNRIGHT PLUNDERES, AND MAY THEY……..

NOT ENJOY……..

WHAT THEY HAVE

APPARENTLY STOLEN.

AMEN!

CHAPTER TWENTY-FIVE

"KARMA – THE MEANING – THE DEED – OR REACTION"

It is the **DOCTRINE** of **EVERY DEED, 'GOOD OR BAD'**, receives **RETRIBUTION,** in view of the events of one's life, combined with the doctrine of **TRANSMIGRATION.** This makes it possible to explain any apparently undeserved pleasure or pain, by the theory that the **KARMA** causing them, was performed in a ***previous existence.***

In all Sects, it remains a ***powerful ethical argument*** used in the stories invented to illustrate it's effects.

It is a work action or **'RITE'** in Hinduism and Buddhism, depicting the idea of **'RETRIBUTION'** in ***the cycle of 'Rebirths,'*** whereby **ACTS OF PREVIOUS EXISTENCIES LEAD TO INEVITABLE RESULTS IN THE SHAPE OF 'GOOD OR BAD' INCARNATIONS IN LATER LIVES.**

Thus the proper performance of duties in **THIS LIFE** will improve one's **FATE** and **STATE** in the **NEXT**. For those who seek release from **TRANSMIGRATION** of souls or from the cycle of rebirths, and also seek attainment of **NIRVANA** – a path of action called **KARMA….. MARGA** is followed. It purposes a life of selfless actions and **'DEBTS** and **DUES'** accumulated in the **KARMA BANK BOOK.**

The doctrine of **KARMA** consists of a **PERSONS' ACTS** and their **ETHICAL CONSEQUENCES.** Human action lead to **REBIRTHS** and **'EVIL DEEDS PUNISHED.'** Underserved pleasure nor unwarranted suffering exists in the world, but rather a universal justice.

The **KARMIC** process operates through the system of ***'Devine Judgment.'*** ***One's*** **KARMA** ***determines such matters as One's Species, Beauty, Intelligence, Longevity, Wealth and Social Status.***

The ethic that leads to **BETTER REBIRTHS** however is ***centered on Fulfilling Ones Duties To Society.*** The precepts prohibit **KILLING, STEALING, HARMFUL LANGUAGE, SEXUAL MISBEHAVIOR,** and the use of **INTOXICANTS.** By observing these precepts, the three roots of **EVIL;** – **LUST, HATRED AND DELUSION** – may be overcome.

So where have **THESE ENEMIES OF HONESTY** planted themselves and their future? The hurts that all my cases in this 'DIABOLICAL' court system can reveal is, the **DISHONESTY** and **SELFISH GREED.** Their one way ticket to the **DEVIL'S ABODE,** has been written many times over for their **TREATMENTS IN MY CASES AND IN OTHERS.**

I, at least, have the knowledge to see their **THIEVERY**. By being Pro Se, I could see first hand their underhanded dealings and their **'DEAL MAKING.'**

Those other **'BATCHES'** of lawyers and judges are already doing time with the rest of the **'CROOKED ESQUIRES'** of the Courts. Their conduct brought them to **DOOM-DOM** for their clients' tear- stained law cases. The **'CHICKENS HAVE NOW COME HOME TO ROOST!'**

For **YOU** who have **HINDERED** and **OBSTRUCTED** the proper and honest decisions in my cases, **YOU HAVE HAMPERED MY JUSTICE, YOU CIRCUMVENTED THE PROPER ADJUDICATIONS, YOU CRIPPLED THE LAW TO FIT YOUR POCKETS.** Now you will see what **YOUR KARMA REWARDS ARE.**

Your life will be filled with abominations. You always looked so sick and disgusting in you **'EVIL BLACK ROBES WITH YOUR GAVEL IN HAND,** as you meted out your **BIASED DECISIONS THAT YOU WORKED OUT IN YOUR CHAMBERS,** beforehand. You were probably guaranteed your **'HANDSOME KICK-BACK' (pay-off)** for your signature on some **'BIASED'** document that compensated you so handsomely ***(by violating statutes, the judge can manipulate the law for his own benefit.)***

Your deceptive conduct and duplicity to your oath as a lawyer and a judge, has earned you this bounty. When you **SUPPRESSED MY TRUTHS** – that gave you **ADDITIONAL DEMERITS. WHAT I WAS A WITNESS TO, IN YOUR COURTS, WAS ORGANIZED HYPOCRISY AND HIGHWAY ROBBERY.**

I have no doubt that you are a **'DISCIPLE'** of some **DEMONICAL ENTITY.** How can you sit on that bench and insult people when you are more **WICKED** and **IMMORAL** and **MALEVOLENT** than anyone could believe?

I now know for sure why I was put into this venue in this last case, Yes, to **SQUARE THE SCORE.** These charlatans who are addressed as **'YOUR HONOR'** wreak havoc in these courts.

THEY JUST DID NOT KNOW HOW TO DEAL WITH ME. I was **THREATENED** and **CAJOLED,** but I fought on. Any lawyer would not dare to disagree with the Judges. They have to be so respectful, after all they are one and the same. **YES, A JUDGE IS NOTHING MORE THAN A LAWYER WITH $50,000.00 TO BUY THE BENCH (judgeship.)**

So now this is **HIS** great prize for delaying justice to the righteous, for **HIS** compensation from **HIS CRONIES.** And now you know what **KARMA** means **'YOUR HONORLESS!'** You will get the same consideration that you gave me and those others who came before you for your – **'HONEST DECISIONS.'**

You who have suppressed the truth are a SHAM, a double dealing **'FLIM FLAM'** artist in the **DEVILS CLOAK.** You **JUDGES** and **LAWYERS** are ***vicious sinners who are toying with peoples' lives when you hand down these*** **'TAINTED MONEY BOUGHT' decisions.**

These BLACK ROBED ONES *with their self-serving decrees have been given the open door to* HELL, *where they can commiserate all through Eternity.* They are automatically ushered in with their names on the **DEVIL'S ROSTER.**

Now, we all know that **TWO PLUS TWO** equals **FOUR; NOT THREE AND A HALF OR THREE AND THREE QUARTERS BUT FOUR**. But in the court system with these Judges **RAPING** the law with their **INTERPRETATIONS and DISCRETIONS,** they have **CARTE BLANCHE** ***to manipulate the laws for their own selfish greed.*** **These DEALMAKERS** are oblivious of the people who come before them seeking **THE JUSTICE** which they deserve.

The die is cast for these '**BROTHERS IN CRIME!'** Their **DESTINY is DOOMED.** Each time they hand down one of their **DISHONEST DECISIONS**, they are sealing their fate. Their **KARMA** is **COMPROMISED FOR ALL ETERNITY.**

They who **SLAY THE TRUTH,** not with a **SWORD,** but with their Judicial Stamp have put their own **NECK** in the **NOOSE,** and remember everything evens out like,,,,,,**2+2=4, AND THAT WILL NEVER CHANGE.**

SO, NOW YOU KNOW WHAT 'KARMA' IS, YOUR HONORLESS ONE,,,,,YOU AND YOUR 'BLACK HIDEOUS ROBE' ARE A SCOURGE ON HUMANITY. NOW AT LAST YOU HAVE THE DEVIL TO PAY, AND CONTEND WITH. LET US HOPE HE WILL BE MORE TOLERANT WITH YOU, THAN YOU WERE WITH ME…

I MUST SAY YOU DID IT YOUR WAY,

AND YOU MOST CERTAINLY EARNED IT,

'YOUR HONOR.'

I AM SURE YOU PROBABLY HAVE

GOTTEN TOP BILLING

IN THE EVIL BOOK SECTION OF

KARMA!!

WITH YOUR NAME

HIGHLIGHTED IN

EXTREMELY BRIGHT NEON

LIGHTS!!!

ADDENDA

After these futile years that I have spent seeking the ever illusive justice in our American Judicial System: **2 cases as a plaintiff WITH attorneys and 2 cases as a plaintiff, a Pro Se (lawyer for myself.)** I have come to this conclusion - seeking justice under the United States law in New York State, is an **ABOMINATION and a PESTILENCE on HUMANITY.**

It is truly a most contrived business for all concerned. The people are like sheep to withstand this **'BLIGHT'** and this **'CURSE.'** These **LAWYERS** and **JUDGES** are a **DISAPPOINTMENT TO MANKIND. I DON'T SAY ALL OF THEM,** but unfortunately the **ONES** who **I HAVE DEALT WITH.**

They will not stop at anything as far as deal making is concerned. Their tactics are truly **DEPLORABLE.** ***A day does not go by that the newspapers do not carry a story about some lawyers doing some awful deal to steal something that is not rightful, and they are getting caught in some nefarious deal.***

In **Joseph Borkin's** Book **'The Corrupt Judge,'** it is filled with such cases about Judge's ***misconduct and dishonesty while serving.*** A sampling of some of ***the Judicial Disobedience*** range from:

Drunkenness, and disregard for terms of statute.

Judges charged with defrauding of Corporations.

Borrowing and using court's money.

Enriching friends and favorite in bankruptcy proceedings.

The payoffs and advances of monies with large law firms and Big Corporations.

Mr. Borkins' book has 310 pages of these misconducts. ***It truly is an enlightenment.*** And this is just a small **SAMPLING** of the subjects in **Mr. Borkins'** book.

NOW WE HAVE MY BOOK. A day does not go by without the newspapers or T.V. news telling about ***some dishonest, disgraceful act*** committed by some judge who ministers **HIS KIND** of law for some kind of pay-off. ***Why is it that they never open up some of those dusty well-lined legal books that always are placed so neatly on their bookcases?*** Maybe, if they opened them once in a while, they might do right by someone instead of **MANUFACTURING THEIR OWN BIASED INTERPRETATIONS,** in order to benefit from some contrived decision, for a lawyer friend.

After all, **WE CITIZENS ARE PAYING THEIR SALARIES WHILE SOME OF THEM SNEER AT US. YES! YES! I HAVE COLLECTED ARTICLE AFTER ARTICLE FROM LEADING NEWSPAPERS** with so many disturbing stories. One article which particularly shocked me was about a judge who was caught ***Masturbating while on the bench, under his*** **'DIRTY BLACK ROBE,'** while ministering, shall we say, some kind of justice in a **LAW ACTION.** The newspaper even printed his picture with the story.

So now little me has to fall into the hands of these charlatans, **HERE, TODAY,** in the courts in our country.

FROM HERE ON.....I TRUST MY CASE TO THE LORD, WHO IS ABOVE THE UNITED STATES SUPERIOR COURTS AND <u>ALL</u> THE JUDGES AND LAWYERS.

BECAUSE.....OUR LORD KNOWS <u>BEST</u> HOW TO DISPENSE JUSTICE!!!

WOULDN'T IT BE WONDERFUL IF WE WAKE UP ONE DAY AND FIND THAT LOVE AND HONESTY AND JUSTICE IS THE RULE OF THE DAY?

IF PEACE AND RESPECT WOULD GOVERN, INSTEAD OF DECEIT AND HARM, BUT UNFORTUNATELY THIS IS NOT A PERFECT WORLD, EVEN THOUGH OUR HOPES AND DREAMS WOULD SO DESIRE IT.

ONE DAY WE SHALL ALL COME TO

REALIZE THAT.........

HONESTY IS THE BEST

POLICY……

AND THE ONLY POLICY….. AND

ONLY THEN. WOULD OUR LIVES

BE SUPREME……HERE ON

EARTH! AND IF EVERYONE WOULD ADHERE TO DOING WHAT IS JUST AND PROPER AND NOT BE GOVERNED BY THE GREED AND SELFISHNESS AND FAVORS, FOR THEIR OWN AVARICIOUS EAGERNESS.

~~~AMEN~~~

CHAPTER TWENTY-SIX

"THE WHITE AND THE BLACK OF IT"

Have you ever thought? There is no difference between a **JUDGE AND A KU KLUX KLANER**, except for the color of **THEIR ROBES.**
The very sight of them in their **BLACK EVIL ROBES,** and those in their **WHITE GHASTLY HOODED SWATHLINGS OF THE KLAN**, ….. makes ……..me…..**SICK!!**

The donning of those rags, give them the **FALSE COURAGE** to carry out their **DEMONIC DUTIES.** It makes them feel like they are **GOD**, and they are all powerful, and that they can make laws to fit their **POCKETS** and **THEIR LIFE STYLE**.

When the **KU KLUX KLANSMAN** burn a cross on someone's lawn, that cross is the symbol of God, they are showing that they defy him. In their **KARMA,** their retribution is well noted. And as for the **BLACK ROBED ONES** who sit in judgment on some legal case of an innocent person seeking his rightful justice, hoping for the **JUDGE'S** gavel and stamp of honesty, without being aware of the **PREDETERMINED DEAL REACHED IN HIS CLOSED CHAMBERS.** ***His hopeful prayers and mercy is compromised.***

So, what is the difference? They both wear robes to cover their sins! One wears **WHITE,** the other wears **BLACK.** They are covering ***sinister evil deadly omens***

Their faces are covered with the **DEVIL'S MASK..** They are **HIS EMISSARY,** here on earth.

These **ROBED ONES** are debased. Their doom is awaiting their departure, and their conduct will be ***recompensed.*** But, it will be ***too late to make amends, too late to undo the work*** they did with the **DEVIL.** Too much ***suffering and tears*** for the hurts they heaped on the innocents.

Now they will be greeted with open arms and glowing fiendish flashing eyes. The same kind of cold ruthless heart like that of **a SPIDER or TARANTULA** who has caught their prey.

They are a gross and depraved menace to humanity, while those sinister **COLORLESS ROBES** they wore on this earth, they should be **INTERRED WITH**.

~ **THE POWER OF THE HUMAN SPIRIT**

IS

TO BE JUST…..

TO BE HONEST…..

AND BE HUMANE…..

AND ….. LET <u>YOUR</u> CONSCIENCE ……

BE <u>YOUR</u> GUIDE

CHAPTER TWENTY-SEVEN

"HOW CAN YOU BEAT THIS SYSTEM?"

At this point I should like to give you some of the sampling of the actual goings on, and the camouflaging of the facts in this case. The duplicity that took place in this court where I was **Pro Se.**

The actual wording from ***The Bona Fide Handwriting Expert*** is as follows: The Expert sent to the Court the ***detailed examination*** and ***comparison*** of ***his findings*** of the **WILLS**…..After studying the submitted documents in extensive detail he observed his conclusion. His exact words are as follows:

"FOLLOWING THE DETAILED EXAMINATION AND COMPARISON OF THE SUBMITTED DOCUMENTS , THE HANDWRITING EXPERT STATES": "THE SAME PERSON WHO SIGNED WILL #1 IS NOT THE SAME PERSON WHO SIGNED WILLS #2, AND #3. WILL #2 WAS DATED (1/19/99) WILL # 3 WAS DATED (1/29/99)"

I then wrote to Judge Fusco to schedule the appearance for the handwriting expert to appear at the **PUTNAM HEARING,** "To give me a date and time frame. It would be a great help, so I could alert the graphologist to appear at the designated time."

Neither the ***Judge*** or his ***assistant*** would give me a time or an approximate time which meant ***the Handwriting Expert*** would have to sit around all day for who knows how long at the **Judge's prerogative**. I not only sent him the Handwriting Expert's conclusion, but presented it in the courtroom and **HE WOULD NOT ACCEPT IT!....**

They made the **TRUTH** an **IMPOSSIBLE DREAM (disclosure.)** ***They did everything to obliterate and disguise the facts in this case.***

ANOTHER EPISODE IN THE SABOTAGING SYSTEM

This is a copy of a letter which was sent to Judge Fusco on April 21. 2001 on the **'ISSUES.":**

At the Putnam Hearing, Mr. Ernest Lombardi testified that **BERNARD** S. admitted to Lombardi, that he is an **ALCOHOLIC**. Yet in the final report on the hearing signed by Surrogate Judge Fusco, **that testimony on alcoholism was completely concealed, as was the identity of the witness Lombardi.**

Issue #1,1

Furthermore, I Gloria Parker, placed two (2) affidavits from different persons at different locations at different times on the Surrogate's Desk. These affidavits attested to **BERNARD'S** arising from his seat declaring: **"I am an Alcoholic….." (Judge Fusco physically rejected the affidavits by pushing them back to me.)**

Issue #l,2

I ALLEGE THAT SURROGATE JUDGE FUSCO PROBABLY CONCEALED COURTROOM TESTIMONY ON DECEDENT'S ALCOHOLISM WHICH CONSTITUTES A CRIMINAL

VIOLATION OF U.S.C. TITLE 18, SECT 3: "ACCESSORY AFTER THE FACT."

"CONCEALMENT," IS A VIOLATION UNITED STATES CODE TITLE 18, SECT 1001 "WHOEVER CONCEALS ---- SHALL BE FINED OR IMPRISONED NOT MORE THAN 5 YEARS OR BOTH"....

"QUESTIONS FOR THE APPELATE DIVISION'

THE SURROGATE JUDGE KNEW THAT TWO PERSONS HAD KEY ACCESS TO DECEDENTS HOME AND THEY ALSO FOUND THE COMBINATION TO THE SAFE CONTAINING MUCH MORE THAN $25,000.00.

DID JUDGE FUSCO CONFRONT THEM IN HIS COURTROOM UNDER OATH, AND ASK EACH IF HE REMOVED CASH FROM THE SAFE HE DID NOT!!!

DID JUDGE FUSCO CONFRONT THEM IN HIS COURTROOM, UNDER OATH, AND ASK EACH IF HE REMOVED CASH FROM THE SAFE? HE DID NOT!!!

DID JUDGE FUSCO INVOKE THE ASISTANCE OF NEW YORK ATTORNEY GENERAL TO SOLVE THIS ROBBERY? HE DID NOT!!!

The two persons were Silvio Marraccini, Esquire, and the decedents trusted neighbor, Anthony Datre.

Marraccini stealthily removed the checkbooks **and financial papers of the decedent, BERNARD.** These might have revealed the cash increments deposited by Decedent between the first, on May 28, 1999, and his death on November 6, 1999.

I requested Marraccini to show me the checkbooks, and he showed only one, with a few entries. BERNARD had told me he had 3 Checkbooks.

The following is an excerpt from the Pre Trial where I, Gloria Parker, questioned the lawyer, Marraccini Under Oath:

Q. Did he (Bernard) check the WILL out? After you wrote it and before he signed it, did he take some time to read it?

A. Yes, he did. He would always take—I would always hold one WILL, whether it be original or copy, and he got a copy or the original, either way. It was one or the other way, and we would go over it.

Q. I can't hear you.

A. We would go over it, Ms. Parker. I would read it to him. He would check it out, yes.

Q. But did he come in with notes about what he wanted you to do it originally like?

A. No. I don't remember notes, no.

Q. So, how did you know what to do?

A. He would tell me verbally, verbally.

Q. **And what happened? How did it come from his mouth to the paper? Did your secretary take the shorthand?**

A. **Oh, no, no, no. Sometimes – who knows if she was around.**

Q. **Well, how did it get from his mouth onto the typewriter?**

A. **I don't even know if she was around when he would discuss things with me. I would make little notes on a pad, a yellow pad. Then after he left I would then call the secretary.**

Q. **And when you made the 2 new WILLS on January 19th. and January 29th. FORGING BERNARD'S SIGNATURE AND LEAVING OUT PROVISION #4 WHEREBY HIS HOUSE WAS TO GO TO HIS CHURCH IN BROOKLYN. THE WILL READS 1,2,3, and 5. Why did you not go back to adjust it and re-number it to make the provisions consecutive?**

A. **You want to know the God's honest truth, I didn't catch them till you caught it. You caught it before me. Yes, that's the truth. I never knew the damn thing was an error otherwise I WOULD HAVE HAD ANOTHER WILL MADE.**

Q. **Well, I'll tell you one thing. I wouldn't let you write a will for me.**

A. **I don't blame you. I won't either for you, but you're right.** ***If I had caught it, I WOULD HAVE DONE ANOTHER ONE.***

Q. **Why didn't you correct it?**

A. ***I didn't catch it. What more do you want? If I had caught it, I would have had her type up another WILL for the lousy one – number four.***

Q. **All right. You're telling me that you knew Bernard for "x" amount of years, you had meals with him approximately several times a month or so, and you didn't know he was an ALCOHOLIC, and that he belonged to A.A.?**

A. **No way.**

Q. **You did not know that?**

A. **Oh yes, He told me about A.A. He told me about it.**

Q. **What about it?**

A. **That he had gone to A.A.**

Q. **Why?**

A. **– YEARS AND YEARS AGO, BECAUSE HE WAS AN ALCOHOLIC YES, HE DID TELL**

ME THAT. MANY YEARS AGO. HE WAS AN ALCOHOLIC.

(~***And I say "Once an alcoholic - always an alcoholic ~And that is why he took advantage of Bernard. Because, Marraccini knowing that Bernard was off sobriety for that short period , took advantage of him. And, going so far as having Bernard's signature forged on those 2 additional wills. They all thought they were going to get away with Bernard's fortune, after all, Bernard had no living relatives to contest all the thievery that was going on. They did not know about me – that I would question these WILLS. They had no idea that they would get caught forging his signature or ransacking and stealing everything from Bernard's home. Although because of the Corruption that reigns in Our Court System – Justice did not prevail. The people who were guilty of crimes got away with it, and did not have to serve any time…..At least not in this world. What goes around comes around and*** **KARMA** ***will follow them for the rest of their lives.***

As for me, I held out for more than they wanted to give me, but certainly not as much as I was originally entitled to. I am glad this NIGHTMARE ON STATEN ISLAND is over because it consumed THREE YEARS OF MY LIFE. I hope by exposing the possible Corruption and the Dishonesty that goes on in the Court System may help you, the readers.)

WITH MY EXPERIENCE, I HOPE ALL YOU WONDERFUL READERS, WOULD BE MOST CAREFUL WHO YOU ENGAGE AS YOUR ATTORNEY BECAUSE WHAT THEY CAN CAUSE YOU, COULD BE DANGEROUS TO YOUR HEALTH AND……….

YOUR WEALTH!........

IT IS MUCH WORSE THAN QUICK SAND AND YOU KNOW WHAT THAT IS. ONCE YOU GET YOUR FOOT IN IT, IT IS HARD TO EXRACATE YOURSELF, AND BEFORE YOU KNOW IT, YOU ARE UP TO YOUR NECK AND OVER YOUR HEAD IN SLUDGE AND FILTH AND THAT IS WHAT HAPPENS WHEN YOU PLAY WITH MUD………

MY BEST WISHES TO YOU ALL. MY PRAYERS ARE WITH YOU. MAY WE ALL SUCCEED IN CLEANSING THESE POSSIBLY MUCK-FILLED, AUSTERE COURTROOMS.

EPILOGUE

Before I close this book, I feel compelled to briefly give a sampling of two other cases prior to this last one where Corruption again reigned in Our Courtrooms.

In the first case, the attorney I engaged, aside from making a play for me, suddenly dropped out in the middle with the excuse he had to have an eye operation. ***(I wonder what his pay-off was to leave me in midstream with this case.)*** Probably a lot of money since the defendant had lots of money and their lawyer had **Big Political Connections.**

THAT is when I found out that the **OTHER SIDE ATTORNEY probably took GOOD CARE OF MY LAWYER to DROP OUT.** So I decided to go **Pro Se. I** kept the case alive for some several years longer with the magistrate Judge who said when we are ready , we would go before the Judge.

Finally he said, ***the time was now for the Judge.*** I was excited, at last we would see some action, because it was quite a case with **Big Adversaries** who made a **National Product.** I had it analyzed in two laboratories and they said it was contaminated with ***Aspergilli's Niger.***

The day arrived to go to court. I got there very early, about **8:30 A.M.,** and to my surprise, there was another lawyer and his staff putting papers and books out all over. He said to me, "What are you doing here?" I said, "My case is scheduled for this morning." He answered, "Impossible, this is an on going case." So I sat and waited for the Judge to come in.

His highness, the Judge, enters the courtroom, sits down on the bench and says, "What's going on here?" I said, "I was scheduled today with my case." The Judge replied, "Could you tell me briefly in a few minutes, what you say happened?" Well I started to tell him, said maybe 4 words and he says, "No, Stop, Miss Parker, I am in the middle of a trial now, and ***I have a Jury coming in,*** and I have to first go over the law with the lawyers in the case on trial. I just don't have a lot of time." So why did he schedule me for that time?

I start to tell him the case and the name of the product, and he asked me to spell it. So I spelled it for him, ***(the name of the product)*** that was involved and the Judge says, "If I were in a spelling bee, I would lose right there."

There was more irrelevant conversation from the bench, a good 8 pages and the Judge says, "Did you try to get a lawyer?" I said, "Yes we had one, but that lawyer had a ***cataract operation."*** He said, "You should really have a lawyer representing you."

This Judge had **ALL** the papers in his hands for the longest time, yet he kept asking me to spell many of the words. He then said, "Don't tell me who it is written by, then you will have to spell it." I want to remind you that he advised me that he had no time for me. He then goes into this diatribe. "You do not have ***4 degrees*** in order to testify as to what went wrong." Then he does an analogy about ***washing machines,*** that has nothing to do with the case. He continued on for **15 – 20 minutes** on how he tried a case on washing machines.

Finally he says – ***"It's going to cost you a huge amount of money to get a lawyer and doctors. They will***

***charge you thousands of dollars, to bring in an expert. I will entertain a motion by the defense for summary judgment, and dismiss this case on notice to you and* I WILL DISMISS IT. DOES THAT SHAKE YOU IN ANY WAY? IS THAT CLEAR?"**

Well you can imagine how I felt. The **OTHER LAW FIRM** a **TREMENDOUS NAME and POLITICALLY CONNECTED,** ***was out to conquer the world , against me.***

So, I bought the transcript. It was **VERY STRANGE. They NEVER HAD IT READY.** They would say, **'CALL BACK TOMORROW."** I will call back the next day, and it still would not be ready. About 8:30 P.M. one night, someone called to say I could pick the transcript up the next day.

When I read it, I was **IRATE.** I decided to send out a **MASS MAILING.** I sent it to **ALL THE JUDGES IN ALL THE BOROUGHS,** about **40 COPIES OF THIS DISASTER.** I wanted other **JUDGES** to see **THIS JUDGE'S THREATS OF DISMISSAL.**

I did not send a copy to the Judge who ***threatened to dismiss my case. I didn't have to. Every other Judge who got the transcript, must have called this creep and said I certainly could represent myself as Pro-Se.***

And for once, I got some satisfaction. **The JUDGE recused himself from MY CASE. So** another Judge now had the case – **HE WAS ANOTHER BROTHER FROM HELL!**

So dear readers – you must know how I fared. I remained Pro-Se , but I did get a Doctor for the case, and I paid plenty. The day of the trial came. The **DOCTOR** held me **UP FOR LOTS MORE MONEY, and DID NOT SHOW UP! After** many meetings with her and giving her a lot of **MONIES**, and **DINNERS**, at the last minute, she was putting the squeeze on me for several thousands more. Obviously, she got a better price from the other side.

In the other most disgusting case in our **'PRISTINE" court system,** I had to endure three years of shear torture. The case made all the papers and even educated me further on the **'Corruption of the Court Systems.'**

My name was given to me by my mother when I entered show business at a very young age. It was **GLORIOUS GLORIA PARKER,** and her all girl Rumba Orchestra. At a very early age, she helped me organize this Latin Band of about nine girls. I not only played the **Marimba** and **Violin,** but fronted this terrific orchestra. We played at some of the finest places including ***the famous Stardust Ballroom.*** We were all very young and still in high school.

Many years later, in the 1990's, a trash novel comes out, which becomes a best seller, wins a Pulitzer Prize, and receives five grants. This book had **NO DISCLAIMOR.** The Author of this book had the audacity to use **MY NAME** and **MY TITLE, "GLORIOUS GLORIA PARKER** and her **ALL GIRL RUMBA ORCHESTRA,"** in it. The author mentioned my name several times throughout the book. **I NEVER** met the man, or knew of him.

One of the episodes in this disgusting book had me standing on the edge of a lake in the Catskill

Mountains at 3 o'clock in the morning, with the moon shining on my blond hair and holding a **DAQUIRI** in ***my hand talking to another male Latin Band Leader saying,*** **"Our Orchestra should be playing together."**

I was in **TOTAL SHOCK**! And I was **FURIOUS!** My family and friends were calling me in disbelief. All my life, throughout my career in show business, my publicity was that **I NEVER** drank alcohol. ***I lived a clean, reputable lifestyle, which was tainted by this disgusting book.*** And the punch line is that **I NEVER WORKED THE CATSKILL MOUNTAINS** in my life.

I contacted a local lawyer to take the case and he asked for **money, money and more money.** The case dragged on for almost 3 years. One day my lawyer contacted me and said to me, ***"Your case has just been dismissed."*** **I NEARLY FAINTED.** How could this be? I never got my day in court. How can someone use my name in a trashy novel and defame my name and get away with it?

Knowing how interlocking Judges and Lawyers on both sides work, I did not pursue this case any further. When the paperback version of the book came out a while later, they changed my name in the book to, **"TINY TEENA MARACAS AND HER ALL GIRL ORCHESTRA."** However, my name remains in the hard cover copy forever....Where is the Justice???

I later found out (shock of all shocks) that the author of "that book" teaches at Hofstra College which is right across the street from the Uniondale courthouse. And, the attorney who he engaged to represent his case, teaches law in the same school. So, all he probably had to do was walk across the street to that infamous courthouse, meet with the Judge…..and …..VOILA…**..THE FIX WAS IN…..**

I OFTEN WONDER, JUST HOW MUCH MY LAWYER PROBABLY RECEIVED TO THROW MY CASE!!!

THEIR CONDUCT IS A CURSE. THE WAY THESE LAWYERS AND JUDGES CHEAT THE PUBLIC, PROVES THAT THEY HAVE POSSIBLY BECOME THE WORST THIEVES. THEY ARE ABOVE THE LAW, BUT THEY ARE NOT ABOVE GOD. SO WHEN THEY STAND NAKED BEFORE THEIR MAKER, AND RECEIVE THEIR JUST REWARDS FOR THE EVIL THEY DO TO GOOD, HONEST PEOPLE THAT THEY HAVE WRONGED, THEY WILL NOT BE ABLE TO BRIBE THEIR WAY, OR MAKE THEIR USUAL DEALS, AND THEY WILL ROT IN HELL FOR ALL THE TRAGEDY THEY CAUSE HERE ON EARTH.

WHAT WE NEED TODAY, IS A BRILLIANT EINSTEIN TO FIGURE THE EQUATION, TO QUELL THIS PLAGUE OF THE VOLCANIC ERUPTION OF OUR AMERICAN COURT SYSTEM, AND TO PUT SOME HONESTY AND LOGIC BACK INTO THE COURTS THAT OUR FOREFATHERS FOUNDED FOR US….
AND THEN WILL WE CELEBRATE WITH JOY AND HAPPINESS ON THAT DAY WHEN TRUE

JUSTICE WILL BE SERVED FOR ALL MANKIND.

TO THOSE OF YOU WHO HAVE SUFFERED UNJUSTLY, LIKE ME, I SAY A LITTLE PRAYER FOR ALL OF US, EACH AND EVERYDAY, THAT THE LORD AND MASTER OF THIS VAST UNIVERSE, WILL IN HIS INFINITE MERCY, GRANT US THE BLESSINGS OF HAVING JUSTICE SERVED ON OUR BEHALF. TO THE ONES THAT HAVE SO UNJUSTLY WRONGED US, MAY THEY FOREVER REPENT FOR ALL THE MISTAKES THEY HAVE MADE. OUR SUFFERING WAS UNNECESSARY AND HURTFUL, BUT INSPITE OF IT ALL, I STILL THINK WE ARE THE WINNERS, BECAUSE

<u>WE</u> HAVE A PURE……..

AND CLEAN HEART AND……..

A CLEAR CONSCIENCE……..

AND WHAT DO YOU THINK THOSE UNJUST LAWYERS AND JUDGES RECEIVED?

ACCORDING TO THE PREACHER…..

THEY HAVE……….

FREE RESERVED TICKETS TO……..

THE BOTTOMLESS PIT……..

OF HELL!!!.......

.
WHERE THEY WILL LANGUISH

FOREVER, WITH THEIR COMPATRIOTS,

WITH WHOM THEY CONSPIRED AND

FACILIATED THOSE POSSIBLY

DEMONICAL AND SATANIC CURSED

DECISIONS FOR THEIR VERY OWN

BENEFIT…………MAY THEY

ENJOY THIS UNHEAVENLY ABODE,

WHICH THEY SO DESERVEDLY EARNED,

FOREVER AND EVER …..

AND INTO …….

ETERNITY!...........

“HOW CAN YOU BEAT THIS SYSTEM?”

How can you beat this system?
A system that is so corrupt
The lawyers and judges have no concern
Their Judicial manners, are most abrupt

You hope to find true justice there
My dear, that is not the way it is done
They have already tailor made their decisions
That is how they kill you, without a gun

The courtroom is a front for their business
The chambers are where the deals are made
And cocktails and dinners for these crooked sinners
That is how their game of “Justice,” is played

So I say- you are nuts to start an action
Unless you are a friend of the Judge, you cannot win
It is a very sad commentary, about the Judiciary
‘Cause their decisions are made solely…..
In sin!

<u>"AND THE LORD SAID"</u> (To the Judge)

"And now that her case is over
Your case is about to.....begin
You will all stand there, before our Beautiful Lord
As he says, "It is here you cannot....come In.

I watched you with your sick manipulations," he said,
"How you twisted and turned all the facts
Your collusions I saw, behind your closed door
All your dishonesty was left, in your tracks

For I am the Lord that rules in these Heavens
The place reserved only for the GOOD and the KIND
And here honesty is the most revered attribute
None of which in you, could I find

I saw those who prayed so hard for your just decision
I saw how you all tragically, massacred the truth
I saw all the unhappiness and suicides you caused from YOUR BENCH
And your backstabbing and double dealing, was most Uncouth.

There are so many demerits attributed to your conduct
`You are the epitome of harshness, you were so rude
And you held that little 'BLOND,' in contempt for NO REASON
Oh Yes, your behavior to her was so very crude.

There is no way of you making it up to your litigants
YOUR EVILNESS has caused so very much Harm
All those monies they spent, caused by your be-Devilment"
The Lord said, "You certainly did cause much Alarm"

All your one-sided decisions did such devastation
You broke EACH AND EVERY LAW, IN MY GOOD BOOK
Your dishonesties and prevarications caused much Reverberations
In my HEAVENS, with THUNDER and LIGHTENING, How it shook
So now comes YOUR day of departure
You have accrued so many demerits on your side
And it seems most odd, as I searched so hard

A candidate to Heaven, you cannot be, qualified

It was your prerogative, to be GOOD and to be HONEST

Then why did you become, so blind sighted

By taking that wrong road, much Evil, you have sowed

And for your dishonesty, you must be severely Indicted.

Your Judicial name, is not to be found on my roster

Because while on the Bench, you did so many –a -Wrong

You are doomed to the Devil for the rest of Eternity

And that is the place you so EARNED, and BELONG.

Gloria.

By: Gloria Parker